CLEARING

HURDLES

A Quest to Be the World's Greatest Athlete

Dan O'Brien and Brad Botkin

Blue River Press
Indianapolis, IN

Cover designed by Phil Velikan
Cover Photos by Randy Bingham of Randy's Vision Photography (leaping) and Vicah Sailer Olympic Photos (standing)
All interior photography is from the private collection of Dan O'Brien
Editorial assistance provided by Dorothy Chambers
Packaged by Wish Publishing

Printed in the United States of America
10 9 8 7 6 5 4 3 2 1

Published by Blue River Press
Distributed by Cardinal Publishers Group
Tom Doherty Company, Inc.
www.cardinalpub.com

This book is dedicated to:

TEAM O'BRIEN:

Mike Keller, Rick Sloan, Brian Tibbitts, Ron Landeck, Michael Joubert, Brad Hunt and Jim Reardon

The coaches who made the difference:

Larry Hunt, Ron Smith, Jess Schefstrom, Lee Schroeder, Harry Mara, Fred Samara and Duane Hartman

The communities who embraced me:

Klamath Falls, Oregon; Pullman, Washington; Spokane, Washington; and Moscow, Idaho

The entire O'Brien family:

Mom, Virginia O'Brien; Dad, Jim O'Brien; Brother and Sisters, Tom, Karen, Patricia, Laura, Sara; Scott Farrar and family; Kathy Fox and family

The love of my life:

Leilani S. O'Brien and our two dogs, Max and Kina

The people that made this book possible:

Tom Doherty (publisher) and Jill Marsal (agent)

The Greats who showed me how to do it:

Bob Mathias, Milt Campbell, Rafer Johnson, Bill Toomey and Bruce Jenner

And all those who seek out meaning and look to inspire others...

As the story goes, when Jim Thorpe won the first decathalon in 1912, King Gustav V of Sweden presented him with the gold medal and said, "You sir, are the world's greatest athlete."

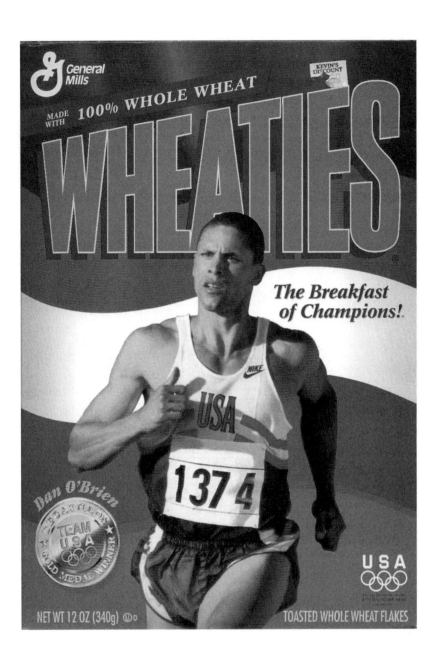

1

> "I must not fear. Fear is the mind killer. Fear is the little death that brings total obliteration. I will face my fear. I will permit it to pass over me and through me. And when it has gone past, I will turn the inner eye to see its path. When the fear is gone there will be nothing. Only I will remain."

I'm a huge science fiction guy, and this, a passage from Frank Herbert's *Dune*, has become my mantra. I've memorized it word for word. And as I make my way onto the practice track on Day One of the 1996 Olympic decathlon, my heart threatening to pound right out of my chest, I seek solace in its message. I close my eyes and remind myself that fear, as paralyzing as it can feel, only exists in our minds. It is controllable, and therefore beatable. It is but one final hurdle on the road to salvation.

I take the deepest of breaths and let it out slowly. My stomach is in knots.

For the last two days I've been an emotional wreck, my anxiety wound tightly enough to snap. I tend to get this way before a big meet. I pace. I fidget. Once in a while I throw up. Some three weeks ago, at the Olympic trials, I laid my head in the lap of my future wife, Leilani, and sobbed for five straight minutes. The stress comes at me like an avalanche, and here, under the crushing weight of the Olympics, in the sticky Atlanta air, it feels all the more suffocating.

Still, I'm careful to walk tall and with a rhythmic strut, projecting an air of confidence, even arrogance. I might be scrambling inside, but I refuse to show it. Not here. Not now. The practice track, especially at a big meet, is a place of intense appraisal. Quietly, we're all watching each other. Sizing one another up. And as has been the case at every track meet I've been to over the past four years, ever since Reebok put out those Dan and Dave commercials that turned me into an overnight celebrity, the attention on me is palpable. Along with Michael Johnson and his unprecedented quest for double gold in the 200 and 400 meters, I'm probably the biggest story here in Atlanta. I'm on billboards all over the country. I'm on the cover of *Newsweek* under a headline that reads "Mr. Olympics." As I jog to get loose, I can feel a thousand eyes following me.

My friend and longtime training partner, Australian quarter-miler Michael Joubert—or "Mick," as we call him—has come to run with me this morning. He does this a lot. Even when he's not personally competing (like, say, at the U.S. Championships), he'll still fly in to run and stretch with me. He knows that in moments of high stress and tension, my greatest comfort lies in my routine.

On this morning, Mick and I do everything, right down to the last detail, as though we're back on the track in Pullman, Washington, where we've been training together just about every day for the past four years. We do hamstring stretches. Butterflies. Modified hurdles. We move through our series of yoga-like maneuvers like clockwork, which allows me to sink into an almost robotic existence. I am willing myself impervious. I tell myself: This is just another meet, just another day at the track with Mick. It's no different. Over and over I tell myself this. *It's no different. It's no different.*

And yet, it is so different.

It's not anything I can put my finger on. It's just something in the air, something about the way Centennial Stadium is looming in the distance like the Roman Coliseum. The Olympic energy is everywhere, and it's making me feel things I've never felt. My mouth is dry. My stomach is hollow. I'm barely 10 minutes into my warm-up and already I'm out of breath. Time and again I've been warned about this exact scenario, told by the likes of Milt Campbell and the great Bruce Jenner that no matter how many major meets I've seen in my life, the sheer intensity of my first Olympic experience was sure to catch me off guard. But only now can I possibly understand what they meant. There's simply no way to prepare for this. No way to know how you're going to react.

For in the words of Bill Toomey, "The Olympics are a complete baptism by fire."

Mick and I jog two laps, always two laps, before settling down at the far end of the track next to the high jump and pole-vault pits, otherwise known as the D-zone. This is where we usually stretch. This is where we stretched at my last world championship, and at this point I'm not at all above superstition. Mick's first Olympic event, the 400-meter, has already passed to the disappointment of his not reaching the finals, and though he still has the 4x4 relay a few days from now, we don't discuss either. Nor do we discuss my impending date with doom—or, as other people like to call it, the decathlon. Right now, I'm doing my best to not even think about this damn thing.

People will tell you, I don't particularly enjoy the decathlon. I never have. In fact, I never wanted to be a decathlete in the first place. I always held out hope that one day I would be the glamorous 100-meter guy, the 29-foot long jumper, the next

Clearing Hurdles

Carl Lewis. I didn't choose the decathlon so much as it chose me. And though it has grown on me over the years, and in many ways has come to represent all that is pure and alive inside me, it's still a love-hate relationship.

A reporter once asked me, "What do you mean by that?"

So I told him, as odd as it sounds, that I love the training. I love the feeling of getting better, getting stronger and faster. I love the work. The sweat. The long grind of the days. Even the pain of training feels oddly good, if not intoxicating. But the actual decathlon is different. A decathlon is the most thorough, most demanding challenge an athlete can possibly face, a true test of both will and skill, and though I love it for this reason, for this opportunity to conquer something so beastly, to become the worthy man, it is also the source of much dread and obsession. I imagine it's a lot like a woman going through labor—you do it for the result, for the indescribable feeling of joy and fulfillment that awaits you at the end. But if getting there isn't miserable, it isn't far off.

I think about the bear jumping on my back down the stretch of the 400m.

I think about the 1500m—the evil fire-spitting monster at the end of the video game.

I think about . . . Demi Moore?

"So?" he says anxiously. "Is she a 10 or what? I'm dying over here."

This is what I love about Mick: He always seems to know just what to say, at just the right moment, to loosen me up in the tensest of times. He knows that I've been getting the red-carpet treatment all week, and that a few nights ago Leilani and I were sitting one suite over from Demi and Bruce Willis when Kerri Strug stuck her famous one-legged landing. We met briefly, both of them wishing me good luck, and now Mick's drooling as I tell him that Demi, somehow, is even hotter in person than she is on her new *Striptease* movie poster.

"Bloody hell," he mutters in his Aussie accent. "Bruce Willis is one lucky bah-sturd."

I should tell you that Mick has a mouth that would make an Alaskan fisherman blush, and much like Bruce Willis, he's short. *Bloody* short. On a good day, in heels, he stands no taller than 5'5". Probably weighs 140 pounds at the most. But make no mistake, with calves the size of softballs and abs like a cobblestone road, he's Popeye yoked. And on top of that, he's certifiably nuts. He usually rocks a Mohawk, though today his head is skinned clean. Both his nipples are pierced. He's got the *No Fear* eyes tattooed on his back. And if he parties like it's his last night on earth, he trains even harder, even crazier, like an honest-to-God madman, pushing himself to such extremes that on more than one occasion I've watched him crumble to the track and break into full-blown convulsions.

When I look at Mick, I see a guy who would kill for what God gave me. He can run, but he wasn't *born* to run. He doesn't have my natural size or power. Everything he's accomplished as an athlete, for the most part, has been in spite of his physical limitations. The man knows no boundaries. Given a choice between quitting and dying, he'd die a million times over. And for me, to train alongside a guy like that has been inspiring. Mick has taught me that in sports, and really, in just about every aspect of life, there are few substitutes for flat out working harder than the next guy.

And trust me, over the last four years, nobody has worked harder than I have.

I feel my adrenaline start to pump, and it lifts me to my feet. It's time to run. Mick and I move back onto the track, where we begin striding down the front straight at half speed, then three-quarters speed, and with every step I take I feel better, looser, my nervous energy releasing like a tight muscle. Between runs I shake out my legs. Bounce on my toes. Roll my neck. I look like a fighter chomping at the bit, as I'm beginning to steel myself for what lies ahead.

I can't feel the eyes of my opponents anymore. Slowly the outside world is fading away. If there's such a thing as a zone, I'm sinking further and further into it. Mick and I have gone from shooting the shit to hardly saying a word. He knows when it's time to leave me alone, and it's time. I'm not interested in anything anyone has to say other than Coach Sloan—the man most responsible for getting me here, the most treasured and trusted voice in my world.

"Thirty-five minutes," Sloan says. "Let's get in the blocks."

This is where Mick and I part ways, and my warm-up becomes very event-specific. The first event of any decathlon is the 100-meter, and the first key to the 100m, of course, is the start. Many races are won and lost inside a nanosecond. I will now come out of the blocks five times over 30 meters, just enough to get my reaction time right. As I kneel into position, backing my feet against the familiar padding, pressing my fingertips against the warm, rubbery surface, Coach reminds me, "Don't anticipate. Listen for the gun." I take my mind 30 minutes into the future. I'm in the Olympics.

Coach says, "Set . . . Bang!"

On the clap of his hands, I explode.

"Lift!" he yells. "Lift!"

He's telling me to get my knees up, to not get choppy. Everything we've ever worked on has to be perfect. There is no room for error today. I'm running tall and proud, with my head high and chest out. I feel good. And with every sprint I feel even better. Coach is a master button-pusher, so between starts he's telling me how great I look, how ready I am, how these are the first of the last few steps in my longest pursuit of destiny.

"Twenty-five minutes," Coach says. "Time for a blowout."

If a sprinter runs three hard intervals during a given workout—and by hard intervals, I mean a legitimate, all-out sprint over at least 100 meters—the second will almost always be his fastest (on the first one he adjusts his body to going full speed over a distance, and by the third one he's a little spent). To me this is common sense, so I've always found it odd that more decathletes don't adhere to this strategy on race day, why they don't get that first hard sprint out of the way on the practice track. When I move all the way back to 150 meters, and everyone looks at me like I'm crazy, like I'm wasting precious energy, it makes me smile inside. I know something they don't.

"Set . . . Bang!"

I come out fast and hard and break into a full-out, 150-meter sprint, and when I come around the turn and push into top gear, it feels as though I've broken free from a pair of shackles. The eyes are back on me, and I like it. Take a good look, motherfuckers. Take a real good look. I fly down the stretch like a rush of wind, my pent-up energy making it feel like I could run forever. It takes all but a parachute to stop me as I cross the line in the neighborhood of 15 seconds. Mick, who's lingering in the area and knows this marks the end of my warm-up, is jacked. The combination of watching me blow out that run and the anticipation of the moment has his already-live wires sparking. As I gather my things, he starts shoving me in the chest trying to pump me up, gritting his teeth and yelling Aussie-inflected obscenities at the top of his lungs.

"Fuck these bah-sturds! They can't fuckin' touch you!"

He goes on and on about how I'm the best, the bloody fuckin' best. He's so juiced that you'd think he's the one who's about to race. I want to share in his excitement, but I know I can't get too pumped too soon. I fight to keep my emotions in check, knowing that the 20 minutes between now and the start of my race will feel like a lifetime.

The call goes out over the loudspeaker: "Decathlon. Heat Three. First call."

That's my cue. The shuttle that will cart us over to the main stadium has arrived. Mick has settled down enough to give me one last hug, and I hold on for an extra split second. Mick and I don't talk much about our friendship, but I hope he knows how much it means to me that he's here. His last words to me are short and sweet.

"It's your time."

I head over for some last-minute instructions from Sloan and Coach Keller. In Sloan I see a man who's been here before, a man who finished seventh in the decathlon at the '68 Olympics in Mexico City. In Keller I see that cold rainy afternoon in the winter of 1988. The day he saved my life.

"You ready?" Keller asks me.

I nod tightly.

My dad says I'm a hard guy to know, a hard guy to love, like my heart is surrounded by some sort of protective moat that keeps anyone from getting too close. If this is true, then my coaches are among the few who have braved the waters. The media likes to quip that in me, Keller and Sloan stumbled upon a broken-down Ferrari, fixed it up, and got it running again. But this is a huge injustice. They've done a hell of a lot more than simply get me running again. They've been through everything with me—through the drinking, through the highs of three world championships and two world records, through the lows of one of the biggest screw-ups in sports history. When so many others had given up on me, they stood by me. Believed in me. And now here we are.

We go over a few last-minute strategies, but really, we don't say much. We don't have to. Mick's right. This is my time. *Our* time. Four years ago we said we were going to win this thing, we promised each other, and I'll be damned if I'm going to break that promise. We've worked too hard, sacrificed too much. Two days from now I will stand on the highest podium in front of my country and listen to the national anthem rain down. It will be the moment I first dreamt about when I was 13, and it will validate everything I've been through along the way. We go through our team handshake, and then, just as I'm about to board the shuttle, Sloan pulls me in close and asks me one last time:

"Are you the greatest athlete in the world?"

I smile. "Absolutely."

It took me a while before I could say that, but now, I believe it with all my heart.

The shuttle looks like something you'd ride from the airport to your hotel. I'm sitting next to Mike Smith, a Canadian decathlete whom I've gotten to know well over the years. You can feel the tension on the shuttle as we move closer to the stadium. Some guys are listening to music. Others are tapping their feet nervously. Me? I'm looking around for a young German by the name of Frank Busemann. He's 21, and he's been lighting the junior circuit on fire. I turn to Mike.

"Which one's Busemann?"

Mike surveys, and when he points out a fresh-faced kid with whitish blonde hair who doesn't look a day out of high school, I can't help but think about my own age. I turned 30 the day I arrived in Atlanta, which is downright elderly in decathlon years. At 28, Bill Toomey remains the oldest decathlete to win a gold medal. Reporters have refused to let me forget this. It seems like every day, when they're not reminding me about 1992 and the pole vault heard 'round the world, they're reminding me about my age.

"Does it concern you?" they ask.

So I tell them no, it doesn't bother me. I don't believe in age. I believe in work ethic and talent, and if you have enough of both, then God's speed. With that said, however, as I look at Busemann and his rosy-red cheeks, I can't ignore the facts. If I'm going to pull this off, I'm going to have to do something that no man my age, in the history of the world, has ever been able to do. My stomach fizzes at the thought.

For the next few seconds I stare at this kid, examining his body language, trying to see into his thoughts. He's got the calmest look on his face—the cocky, almost apathetic look of a kid who doesn't know any better, a kid who's blissfully naïve to the magnitude of the moment. He must feel the weight of my stare, because suddenly he turns, and for the very briefest of pauses, we lock eyes. He smiles, nods, and immediately turns away.

I think to myself, *Jesus, I don't scare this kid one bit.*

And to be perfectly honest, despite my apparent fixation, Frank doesn't scare me, either. Three years ago I started working with Dr. Jim Reardon, a sports psychologist who very quickly turned into my life therapist. We've spent countless hours talking about countless things. And if I've learned nothing else during that time, if I've discovered no answers that pertain to this fear I'm feeling right now, I've at least discovered that it runs far deeper than any baby-faced opponent could ever reach.

We pull up to the stadium, where dozens of volunteers in white Polo shirts are trying to keep the scene organized. Hundreds of fans are milling around the athletes' entrance, and the moment I get off the shuttle, people start jockeying for position, yelling my name and reaching across the rope with programs and pens. Usually I'm one to sign autographs until my hand cramps, but today I move right past people. By now I've transported my mind to a place of such intense focus that everything around me has turned to a muffled white noise, like I'm inside my own little bubble, everything happening on the periphery. When guys wish me good luck beneath the stadium, I just nod and keep right on walking. I hardly even look up.

Just beyond the drug-testing area is a stretch of track about 80 meters long. That's where I head. I want to keep moving. Keep the blood flowing. After a few sprints I make my way to a section of TV monitors to watch the first 100-meter heat. I walk up beside Steve Fritz, one of the three American decathletes at these games.

He says to me, "How you feeling, OB?"

I barely even hear the question. I just nod toward the television hanging on the wall. "Where we at?"

"First heat's just about to start."

Fritty's a big, strong, All-American-looking guy and a hell of a decathlete. He played hoops at Kansas State, and since turning his full attention to the decathlon, his marks have gotten consistently better. He's recently added five feet to his shot and 10 feet to his discus, and most impressively, he's trimmed almost a half second off his hurdles. Some people think he's got a realistic shot to medal. Perhaps the same could be said of fellow American Chris Huffins, who we just watched run 10.47 in the 100m. It's a good time, but for Huffins, who just a few weeks ago at the trials set the decathlon 100-meter record with a time of 10.22, it's just average. I know I can beat it. At those same trials, inside this very same stadium, I ran 10.3, and my personal best is 10.23, the second lowest time in decathlon history.

But I also ran 10.7 just a week ago in a track meet over at Life College. A bunch of guys went to this meet just as a way to stay fresh leading up to their events. I didn't think anything of it until I saw that 10.7 pop up. Now I've been trying to forget it ever since. Now I'm wondering, "What if my speed just isn't there today?" This is no time for even the slightest inkling of doubt. As I jog back toward the tunnel, I think about Bruce Jenner and his famous pre-race saying: *Feet don't fail me now.*

I hop onto a training table, my feet dangling as I close my eyes and begin a series of deep, diaphragmatic breaths, pushing my stomach out as I inhale slowly, deeply, thus dropping my diaphragm and allowing my lungs maximum room to expand. I've become a huge believer in the power of meditative breathing and positive imagery. Over the years Dr. Reardon has helped me to create a mental highlight reel, a slideshow of my fastest runs, my highest jumps, my most powerful throws, and as I continue with my breathing, I close my eyes and begin watching. I see my 400-meter in Tokyo. My shot put in France. I visualize myself flying over a seven-foot bar, bounding over hurdles with ease, pulling away from the pack over the last 20 meters.

And then I hear it. That deep Texas drawl I know so well.

"All right, boys. Time to get it goin'. Follow me."

It's Shirley Crowe, the USA Track & Field official who has ushered me up the tunnel at just about every major meet over the last six years. He's wearing his usual cowboy hat, and his familiar voice snaps me back into the moment. I hop down from the training table and begin bouncing on my toes. Just as I go to enter the tunnel, Shirley stops me and puts his massive arm around my neck. He says he knows he's not supposed to play favorites, but he's been watching me for such a long time.

"You're the best, son," he says. "We're all rooting for you."

Thanks, Shirley.

"Now go out there and give 'em hell."

I'll see what I can do.

As I begin the long, slow walk up the tunnel, which is brightly lit and eerily quiet, I try to remain calm. I tell myself to relax. But how do you relax when it's all you can do to breathe?

13   Clearing Hurdles

I hear the track announcer in the distance, feel the vibrations in the concrete walls. I try to ignore it all. Try to stay in this bubble of mine. But everything is getting louder, moving faster. And then, all at once, reality comes crashing into me like a wrecking ball.

Holy shit! This is really happening! I'm in the fucking Olympics!

I find I'm so excited that I can hardly hold a thought in my brain. But my excitement isn't alone. It's mixed with equal parts nerves and anxiety and a tiny bit of scared shitless. There's a cocktail of emotions splashing around my stomach, and my only recourse is to clench my jaw and stare straight ahead, my whole life flashing before my eyes. It feels as though the cold musty walls are closing in around me, and when I spot Dr. Reardon in the distance, he can see in my eyes that I'm scrambling. I go to him like a port in high seas.

"Be present," he reminds me.

He massages my shoulders and calls me Champ.

"Stay in the moment," he says. "You're ready."

He's right. I am ready. I've done everything in my power to prepare for this day, and I should find strength in that. Courage. I land on a moment of clarity, confidence, but then it's gone again, almost as though I'm moving in and out of consciousness, sounds turning into silence and silence back into sounds. As I near the end of the tunnel, there's a cameraman with a long boom mic zeroing in on me. I try to ignore it as the morning heat whooshes against my face.

A baptism by fire.

The official gets a call on his walkie-talkie. "OK, boys, you're up."

To try to explain the surge of adrenaline I'm feeling in this moment would be next to impossible. My whole body is tingling. My heart is racing. But I have to admit, as I walk onto the track and take my first look around, I'm a little disappointed. Here I am in this giant stadium that seats close to a hundred thousand people, and I bet there aren't more than ten thousand fans scattered all over the stands.

This is the non-glamour of the decathlon. Like a triathlon, it's almost as arduous to watch as it is to actually do. It's nine in the morning and starting to mist. Most people are still sleeping. Later tonight, when Carl Lewis is long jumping, when the glamour events are going off, this place will be packed to the gills. When I'm running the 400-meter, the whole world will be watching. But right now, I must embrace the internal quest of the decathlon.

I don't look for my coaches or my family. I squeeze my focus until it's airtight. I strip off my warm-up pants. It's getting close. Only a few moments now. I check my uniform, tightening the corners of my number and adjusting my shoelaces just so. Michael Jordan believes an athlete plays the way he looks, and who am I to argue with Jordan? I take my position in Lane 8, right next to Busemann, and in a weird way, everything is starting to slow down. Few people ever come face to face with their dream, but here I am, and I find that there's a certain calm in knowing the chase is almost over. If I can just get through these next two days, maybe, just maybe, I can finally stop running.

Clearing Hurdles

100-Meter

I position myself in the blocks, pressing my fingertips firmly against the track, just as I did 20 minutes ago with Sloan. Only now my psychology has reversed. When I was on the practice track, I imagined I was in the Olympics, but now that I'm in the Olympics, I'm imagining I'm on the practice track. I take a deep breath and everything goes quiet. My world shrinks to the beating of my heart and the sound of Coach Sloan's voice in my head. Don't anticipate. React. Listen for the gun.

I feel like a loaded spring.

Set . . . Bang!

Busemann gets a great start, and he's got me by a stride for the first 50 meters. But then I begin to close. And close. And now I'm pulling ahead. This is the thing about the 100-meter—it's a longer race than you think. The fastest man almost always has time to prevail. And today, at least in my heat, I am the fastest man. I run 10.5 seconds, second only to Huffins' 10.47. It's not the time I was hoping for, not the time I'm capable of, but it's good enough to get me started. I can work with it.

Before I can head back under the stadium to rest up for the long jump, I have to go through the mix zone, which is basically a swarm of media people with microphones and tape recorders and a whole bunch of television cameras. I get questions from all the local and national reporters before Chris Collinsworth, the old Cincinnati Bengals receiver, pulls me aside for NBC. He asks me three or four questions before bringing up the 10.47 Huffins ran to assume the early lead. When he asks me how I feel about that, I tell him simply, "There's a long way to go."

There was a long way to go, indeed.

Dan at age 1

2

My original birth certificate confirms that I was born on July 18, 1966, in Portland, Oregon. In addition, it lists my mother's maiden name as Westcott, her race as Caucasian and her place of birth as New York City. My father's information, on the other hand, has simply been left blank. Sadly, this is the reality for many adopted kids: a lot of blanks. And the worst part is, unless you end up meeting your birth parents, unless you actually sit down and hear it from the horse's mouth, you can never be totally sure if those blanks are being filled in accurately. Even the things your foster parents tell you are merely an echo of what they've been told, and what the person before that was told, and we all know how stories can spiral. I'll never forget the time I read in a magazine article that my biological father was suspected to have been a famous athlete.

If this is true, it's news to me.

So this is my disclaimer. When it comes to the parts of my life I can't remember, I can make no absolute claims of what is or isn't true. I can only tell you what I've been told. And from what I've been told, my name wasn't always Dan. As the story goes, I was first taken in by a lady who named me Wesley, but she only dealt with newborns and infants, so about a year later I was transferred to a group orphanage in Portland called Waverly Children's Home. There I was given a different name. Dion.

It was 1967 when I went to Waverly as a biracial, mocha-skinned baby, and the world was a different place. To adopt outside your own race was considered taboo, and in some places—like Medford, Oregon, for instance—it wasn't even legal. Lucky for me, Jim and Virginia O'Brien (both of whom were white) didn't live in Medford. They lived about an hour's drive east, just north of the California border in an old timber town called Klamath Falls. A few years earlier they'd gone through Waverly to adopt a little Native American girl named Karen, and now they were in the market for another.

My mom tells the story like this: "They asked us what type of child we were looking for, and we told them that we weren't picky. We would take whatever they had."

"Great," the orphanage people said. "We've got a happy little half-black boy who just celebrated his second birthday. Why don't you guys come up and have a look at him."

So that's what they did.

Even though I was barely two years old at the time, I can still remember the day Jim and Virginia O'Brien picked me up from Waverly. I remember that they brought Karen with them, and that she and I went off to play while the adults "talked." Apparently this was when a few more details about my past were revealed—namely that my parents were a young college couple when I was born, and that my father, though nothing but a blank spot on my birth certificate, was in fact a tall, athletic-looking black man.

Meanwhile, Karen and I were off playing. I remember that she was making me giggle by poking me in the stomach. We were having fun. I think she liked me. And when the adults came back, I remember her pleading with my mom, tugging at her pant leg and asking, "Can we keep him? Can we? Can we?"

My mom looked down at her with a soft smile and said, "We'll see."

I remember those words specifically. *We'll see.*

I didn't realize it at the time, but this day, essentially, was my tryout.

I'll never forget going to the Portland Zoo that day, where I was deathly afraid to get a drink of water because the fountain rested inside a huge plastic lion's head. I can still see myself, a sort of vague, faded picture in the back of my mind—my mom holding me up to the fountain, her arm wrapped firmly around my waist, my feet dangling as she assures me the lion won't bite. I trust her, and the water splashes cool against my lips. When she puts me down, I take hold of each of my soon-to-be parents' hands and continue walking around the zoo. Every once in a while they swing me off the ground and I giggle with a pure, safe glee. With Karen walking alongside, it is my first taste of family.

"Still," my mom would tell me years later, "we weren't sure about keeping you."

"Why not?"

To make a long story short, my dad was nervous about the idea of adopting a biracial baby in Klamath Falls, which was a very rural, old-fashioned community with almost no black people. Remember, this was during the wake of the Civil Rights Movement. People were still warming up to the idea of blacks and whites commingling, never mind living under the same roof. My dad feared the situation would be hard on them as parents, and maybe even harder on me as the kid. They sat down on a park bench to talk about it. I sat at their feet and amused myself.

This I don't remember.

According to my mom, somewhere in the middle of their conversation I crawled up in my dad's lap, laid my head against his chest, and fell fast asleep.

"And that was all it took," my mom says. "Your dad's heart melted right there. He just looked down at you and smiled and said, 'I can't give him back. This is my boy.'"

Shortly thereafter, I was given my third and final name. Daniel Dion O'Brien.

And so there I am, pulling up to a new house with a new name in the middle of a new town. My parents walk me inside and show me to my bedroom. My very own bedroom! A few days later I'm out in the backyard playing, and my dad is dumbfounded. He can't believe that he can already see my calf muscles when I run, or that I'm jumping on and off the picnic table at an age when most kids are simply trying to stay upright. He calls for my mom to come outside and have a look. He calls me Speedy Gonzalez.

"You've got to see this kid!" he exclaims proudly. "He's Olympic material!"

My mom, forever the voice of reason, my early Bruce Jenner, chuckles and rolls her eyes. "Is that right?" she says sarcastically.

"I'm telling you," my dad says. "We got the one in a million."

For a while it's just Karen and me, and I think she walks on water. She's my big sister. I mimic her every move and do whatever she says. One day she tells me to close my eyes and open my mouth, and when I do she drops a black spider on my tongue and runs off laughing. A precedent in my life has been set. From this day forward, I will be a follower. I will wait for others to take the lead, and then go quietly along with whatever they say. I don't want to ruffle any feathers. More than anything in the world, I just want people to like me. And I harbor a deep, dark fear that they don't.

Dan and Karen

In the second grade I start taking the bus to school, and there's a cast of bullies who always sit in the back. Every day they call me half-breed and laugh as they take turns punching me in the arm, leaving monkey bumps on my thin skin. My eyes fill with water every time, and I know I can't go on this way. I'm starting to have nightmares about getting on the bus. So one day, in my most desperate voice, I turn to the ringleader and say, "Why are you always being so mean to me?"

He gets a devilish scowl on his ugly face. "Because I don't like you," he says.

It's the worst thing I can hear, and I'll do anything to change his mind, even if I have to do things I don't want to do, things I know are wrong and mean. One time I supply the eggs for their weekend house-egging spree, and in a begging attempt to fit in with these punks, I even throw a few myself. But it doesn't work. Come Monday, they still harass me. Still punch me and laugh. So a few weeks later, in a last-ditch effort to make peace, I offer to bring the kid 10 dollars if he promises to leave me alone. When he agrees to the deal, I run home after school, steal 10 bucks out of my mom's wallet, and the next day I pay the kid off.

We even shake on it.

And at this point, I'm not just paying this shithead off for me. I'm also paying him off for the mean things he says to Patricia, my new little sister. Patricia, like me, is mixed-race. My parents brought her home when I was four, and shortly thereafter, when I was six, we got a two-year-old Hispanic boy named Tom, the fourth O'Brien adoptee and the little brother I'd always wanted. One day I asked my mom the obvious question, why she and my dad decided to adopt so many kids, and her reason was simple:

"Your father and I are spiritual people, and we believe this is our calling."

By the time I've reached the fifth grade our number has grown to six, with the newest additions being two Korean girls named Laura and Sara. To make room for everyone, my parents have moved us 10 miles outside town, to the thick of the Klamath country, where we live in an old converted barn on 12 acres of farmland that backs up to the Lost River. To me, it's a young boy's paradise— a sanctuary of rope swings and swimming holes and

The O'Brien kids: Dan, Tom, Laura, Karen, Sara and Patricia

wide-open spaces. I go fishing for steelhead. I ride dirt bikes and dune buggies. But I also have a list of chores that could break a grown man's back.

For the rest of my years at home I will spend countless afternoons hauling and laying sprinkler pipe, building fences, picking alfalfa, bucking hay, painting sheds, even putting on the occasional bee suit to collect honey from our hundreds of beehives. In the dead of winter, when I'm splitting and stacking firewood in the snow, when my feet and hands are frozen numb, I will long for the day when I won't have to work so hard. But my mom says no such day is coming.

"You better get used to it, buddy boy," she tells me. "You're going to be working for the rest of your life."

My dad makes a decent living with the forest service, but with all the mouths we've got to feed, we cut every corner possible. Hand-me-down clothes. Old shoes. No summer camp. To trim our grocery bill my dad has filled our property with beef and dairy cattle and a whole mess of chickens, so now you can add gathering eggs and plucking feathers to my list. The first time I see a cow get slaughtered is brutal. They press a .22 rifle right between her eyes and pull the trigger, and a few days later our freezer is so jammed full of meat that you can hardly close to door.

Another thing we do to save money is travel at odd times, avoiding the spike of the summer prices. My mom has two kids from a previous marriage—Scott, who lives just outside Klamath Falls in a town called Keno, and Kathy, who has moved with her family to Los Angeles' San Fernando Valley. One year we take a week off school in the middle of winter and go down to stay with her and my cousins.

My dad yells, "Who's ready to go to Disneyland!"

We all cheer, and a few minutes later we're chugging out of town on Gulliver.

Gulliver is an old, run-down school bus that has been turned into the ultimate camper. It has bunk beds and a wood stove and a foldout table for dinner. My dad has named it after the children's book, *Gulliver's Travels*, even painting the word GULLIVER in big block letters down the side—as if we need any help drawing attention to ourselves. We're a big family. A loud family. By the time we pick up Scott and Kathy and their families, and my dad's brothers and sisters and all their kids, we're rolling down the highway almost 40 strong, everyone laughing and cheering and singing the song that will forever be stuck in my head.

Jesus loves the little children
All the children of the world
Black and yellow, brown, red and white
They're all precious in his sight
Jesus loves the little children of the world

If you know this song, you'll notice the addition of the word *brown*. When listing the different colors of the children, the real lyrics say "black and yellow, red and white," but my mom has added *brown* for my Hispanic brother, just so he won't feel left out. She's always doing little things like this, going long out of her way to assure us of our place in the family—because she knows that none of us, especially the newest kids, are entirely comfortable with that yet. One night she'll make a classic Asian meal just for Sara and Laura. Another night she'll do a Mexican dish for Tom, tacos or enchiladas with homemade hot sauce.

"It's important to take pride in where you come from," she tells us.

For me, she wants me to understand what it means to be black. She tells me what little she knows about slavery and Dr. King and the fight for civil rights, the basics, and for the rest she puts me in front of the TV to watch "Roots." She even warns me about all the nasty names people might call me one day, names like nigger and monkey. She forgets about half-breed, so I add that to the list.

"But these are just names," she says. "And what do we say about names?"

Sticks and stones.

"That's right. Sticks and stones. Don't ever be ashamed of the color of your skin."

She says this, but at the same time she has also told her own mom, my grandma, who comes from the old school and would never approve of her daughter adopting a black kid, that I'm Puerto Rican.

"Just until she gets to know you," she says.

And this is the contradiction of it all. There's everything you're told, and then there's everything you see and feel, everything that's *real*. My mom says we're no different than any other family, but that's not the truth. The truth is that we look like the brochure for It's a Small World, and people look at us funny. When we're all standing in line for a ride at Disneyland, a man asks me if we're some kind of tour group. He saw us pull in on a bus. He's asking me what our story is when I don't even know *my* story.

"No, we're not a tour group," I tell him. "We're a family."

I say it firmly, convincingly. But which one of us am I trying to convince?

My mom's no dummy. She knows this adoption-thing is no cakewalk. She knows that just beneath all the singing and laughter is a bunch of fragile, scared kids who are trying to find their footing like a rookie ice skater. I sometimes think it might be easier if I were the only adopted kid in an otherwise established family. You know what I mean? Maybe then I could latch onto something firmer.

Or then again, maybe that would only make me feel more on my own.

It's confusing, I think, for all of us, and my mom gets that. She's enlisted the services of a family therapist, a pastor from our church who comes to the house a few times every month, but personally, I never really open up about anything. If I did, I think I would tell him how weird it is that a kid can feel so alone even though he's constantly surrounded by people. And I might bring up this idea that my own grandma might not like me, as this only serves to confirm my greatest insecurity: that no matter how hard I try to break in, I will always be just a little bit on the outside.

I imagine my siblings feel the same way. How could they not? We've been thrown together and told we're brothers and sisters, but are we *really* brothers and sisters? We don't look like each other. In some cases, we've only known each other for a few months. Our plight is our bond, yes. But if I'm being totally honest, I think we all feel a little bit like that random piece of a jigsaw puzzle that you have to sort of force into fitting. You convince yourself that it works because you want it to, because you *need* it to, but deep down, in your heart of hearts, you can't help but wonder if that piece, in fact, belongs somewhere else.

3

I'm 11 years old the time I first taste victory. It's a Saturday afternoon, and my dad has taken me to the homecoming festivities over at Merrill High, a small high school just outside Klamath Falls. Before the football game there's a big parade and all kinds of fun contests for kids, one of which is a one-mile race called the Run for Fun. Around the schoolyard I've become known for my speed, but this is a chance to run in front of what feels like the entire town. This is big. I can't get to the start line fast enough.

The announcer says, "On your mark, get set . . . Go!"

I take off like I'm shot out of a cannon (or at least this is what it feels like), and while other kids are probably just doing what the race title says and running for fun, I go straight to the front, which is an instinct I'll never lose. The race has begun on the first turn of the track inside the stadium, and it's tight for a second. But by the time we exit the stadium and move out onto the winding cross-country-type path that makes up the middle portion of the course, I've pretty much pulled out of sight. Only one kid is keeping pace with me. We move stride for stride through the evergreen shadows, and as we crest a small hill and circle back into the stadium, I push into high gear and begin pulling away from him like he has the brakes on.

By this time the stands are packed for the game. Hundreds, if not a thousand people rise to their feet and begin cheering me down the homestretch, which thrills me in a way I find hard to describe. For maybe the first time in my life, I don't feel even the slightest bit insecure. I don't feel nervous or unsure of myself. I'm just running, and it feels right. The whole world feels right. As the cheering builds to a crescendo, so does my adrenaline, and when I cross the finish line first and throw my hands in the air, it's a feeling I wish I could bottle up and save forever.

And the winner is . . . Danny O'Brien from Klamath Falls!

My dad snaps a picture as they present me with a big blue ribbon, and for the pride I feel, it may as well be a gold medal. Everyone circles around and congratulates me.

One guy says, "Dang, son, where'd you learn to run like that?"

I shrug my shoulders and smile, not even embarrassed about the gap in my teeth, then I glow the whole ride home. I run inside the house, yelling, "Mom! I won! I won!" She's in the kitchen making dinner, and she looks tired. These days, she always looks tired. The demands of a big house and even bigger family are wearing on her. But my ribbon makes her smile. She bends down and gives me a hug, tells me she's proud of me.

"You should've seen it," I say excitedly. "Everyone was yelling and cheering for me at the end."

"Like a little Seabiscuit," she says.

"What's a Seabiscuit?"

"Seabiscuit was a great racehorse," she explains. "And Lord how the people cheered for him."

She goes on to tell me the story of the day Seabiscuit raced against War Admiral in the Race of the Century. It was 1938. Depression time. And Seabiscuit, who had never really outgrown his underdog status, had become everyone's symbol of hope. Fans came from all over to watch the race, and my mom, like millions of other people around the country, sat with her dad and listened on the radio. War Admiral was considered unbeatable, but as it turned out, he wasn't. Seabiscuit beat him. And the crowd roared.

"People want a reason to cheer, Danny," Mom says. "And Seabiscuit gave it to them."

I'm a complete sucker for sappy movies with Hollywood endings, so this story has my skin popping with goose bumps. It's the perfect cap to what has been the perfect day. I've been introduced to the thrill of hearing people cheer for me, and now I'm addicted. I want people to like me. I'm secretly desperate for it. And oh, how the spotlight shines warm when you're doing something you're good at. I sleep all night long clutching my blue ribbon.

My Little League baseball team is called Klamath Construction. I'm an OK player, if only because I'm fast and pretty decent at catching fly balls. But I'm an awful hitter, and I don't have anyone to help me get better. My coaches are just parents trying to help out, and my dad, though he played some football in his day, isn't exactly a baseball savant. One time he subbed for the field umpire at one of my games, and on a close play at first, he cocked his fist high in the air and screamed "Safe!" at the top of his lungs.

Uh, dad, you've got that backward. A cocked fist means "out."

So, in light of my lacking baseball tutelage, I take it upon myself to learn the ways of the game. I become a master imitator. I watch the better players on my team and the guys on TV, paying close attention to their every movement, most notably where and how they stand and when they start their swing, because it always seems like I'm behind the pitch. I beg my dad to buy me one of those poles that stick in the ground with a Wiffle ball hanging from a string. I hit on it every day, the ball swinging round and round like a tetherball, and the next thing you know I'm one of the best hitters on my team, helping to save our perfect season with a game-tying hit with two outs in the bottom of the last inning.

It has been said that the ability to learn quickly, the ability to hear or see instruction and apply it shortly thereafter, is the truest measure of potential. If this is true, then a degree in engineering, in all likelihood, is not in my future. You could teach me fractions every day for the next 20 years and I still wouldn't get them. But when it comes to sports, I'm a fast learner. Show me something once and I've generally got it, as matters of the body just seem to make sense in my head. One day I find an old rusty golf club and a handful of balls in the shed, and though I've never swung a club in all my life, I send the very first shot the length of our property, which is well in excess of 200 yards. I don't know how to explain it, but things like that just come easy to me.

I guess you could say I'm physically smart.

And that's what I love most about guys like Julius Erving and Broadway Joe and the acrobatic Drew Pearson—they make everything look so easy, so natural. They're more than just athletes. They're showmen. Entertainers. That a man can single-handedly bring fifty thousand people to their feet is mesmerizing to me.

"Someday," I often say, "someday, that's going to be me playing on TV."

Whenever I say things like this, my mom, like all mothers trying to protect their kids from disappointment, is always quick to bring me back to reality.

"Only 1-in-10,000 people makes it to the pros," she says.

Don't ask me where she gets this statistic, but she's sure of it. One in 10,000.

"If I were you, I wouldn't get my hopes up."

She doesn't say this to be mean or discouraging, it's just that this is more her style. That Seabiscuit story? That was out of character for her. She doesn't share my romantic, dreamy head. That's my dad's department. He's an amazing artist, and I know he dreams of one day doing something big with his pictures. But my mom lives in what she likes to call the "real world." And in the real world, people grow up and get jobs.

"It's just the way it is, honey," she tells me. "Games are for kids."

It sticks square in my craw when she says this, and proving her wrong, in a way, has become my first real motivation in life. Sports are my ticket. My chance in life. I know this even as a little boy. Each week I beg my mom to let me watch Monday Night Football on the big TV in the living room, but in my house, majority rules when it comes to the big TV. And with five girls all casting a vote, I don't stand a chance.

"You know the rules, Danny."

I know, I know. Mondays are for that dumb show "Little House on the Prairie." If I want to watch the game, I have to go upstairs and watch it on the tiny, rabbit-eared, black-and-white Zenith that I have to hit to unscramble the picture.

And so I go, every week, off to my home within my home and the soothingly familiar voice of Howard Cosell. If the dreamer in me has already been born, then it is here, in this room, in front of this TV, watching the Cowboys and Steelers and Ali's Rumble in the Jungle, that it really begins to take

Clearing Hurdles

shape. I know the stats of every Dodgers player by heart. Dusty Baker and Davey Lopes are my guys. When Reggie Jackson hits three homers in Game 6 of the '77 World Series, it's the cruelest night ever. I hate the Yankees. I root for the underdog, maybe because that's how I see myself.

Speaking of underdogs, it's February 22, 1980, and the U.S. hockey team is about to square off against the almighty Russians. Like everyone else in America, I've fallen head over heels in love with this team. I've watched every second of every game during this crazy run through the Olympics, and tonight my parents have given me the greatest gift of all time by letting me watch the game on the big TV.

I flip it on just in time to hear Al Michaels' intro, and from the opening face-off, I'm on pins and needles. The Russians are a juggernaut, winners of the last three gold medals. We lost to them a few weeks ago by almost 10 goals, but it's a new game. Hope has been restored in the mantra that anything, on any given day, can happen. I'm hanging on every shot like it's life or death, and when Mike Eruzione's shot finds the net to give the U.S. a 4-3 lead with just over 10 minutes to play, I come out of my chair like I'm strapped to a rocket.

But there's still a lot of time on the clock. Ten minutes. A lifetime.

I hunker down, flinching every time the Russians shoot. I'm sure they're going to score. They're too good not to. Pucks are flying at Jimmy Craig like a game of Asteroids, but he's a wall. He's blocking everything.

My sister barges in. "Can we change the channel?"

Are you kidding! Get out of here!

Seven minutes to go. Six minutes. Five minutes. The clock seems to be ticking in slow motion, but you can feel the anticipation rising. Are we really going to pull this off? I would've never believed it, but Craig is still holding strong. And now we're down to two minutes. One minute. I hold my breath for the last 30 seconds, and then, finally, I hear it.

"Do you believe in miracles!"

The crowd goes absolutely bonkers as the players spill onto the ice, their sticks and gloves flying in the air, and in this moment, it feels as though the entire country is cheering. I can't take my eyes off the TV. I can't stop thinking about what it would be like to be in the middle of that celebration. Not in the stands, but on the ice, in uniform, the letters USA written across my chest. For a kid who always longed to feel like a part of something—like a real, true part of something—it would be the ultimate.

My mind is made up. I turn to my dad and say, "I think when I get older I'm going to be in the Olympics."

I don't have to make a believer out of him. He's believed in me from the start.

"In what event?" he asks.

Oddly, I've never considered this question. I've never bothered to ask myself what my favorite sport is. I love them all. I'll play anything anytime anywhere, just as long as I'm playing something. But now my dad's putting the heat on, and I'm taking the question seriously, as though I'm going to be contractually bound to this decision for the rest of my natural life.

If you're going to go to the Olympics, what will be your event?

"Man, that's a tough one," I sigh. "I can't decide."

A decathlete from the start.

Clearing Hurdles

Our childhood home

The O'Briens: Sara, Karen, Dan, Patricia, Laura, Tom, Jim, Virginia and Pip

Long Jump

The greatest long jump I ever saw came at the 1988 Olympic Trials in Indianapolis. It had suddenly started dumping rain, like the bottom had fallen completely out of the sky, and everyone was scattering for cover. Except Carl Lewis. As the other athletes stood beneath umbrellas and awnings, Carl stood unfazed at the end of the runway, the rain pouring down on him in sheets, a look of complete stone on his dripping-wet face. The rain pounded. And pounded. And Carl just kept staring down that runway. I couldn't take my eyes off him. Nobody could. I thought to myself, Is he seriously going to jump in this shit?

Never in my life have I seen somebody so locked in, so impervious to his surroundings, so totally committed to the task at hand. The rain had absolutely no power over him. He motioned to the judge in a way that said, "One jump. That's all I need." Then he takes off down the runway, and every eye in the stadium follows him. He picks up speed, and more speed, and more speed. He explodes off the board, and for me, it's all happening in slow motion. He sailed over the pit, his legs cycling in classic fashion, as though he was running on air, and when he slammed into the sand with a full-hitch landing, he knew it was good. He looked for the mark. 28-9. A monster jump. Then he casually picked up his things and walked off the track. Didn't say a single word. As the rain crashed down with a thunderous force, you could literally feel the jaws of his opponents hanging.

Before the competition had even started, it was over.

I turned to Coach Keller and say, "I guess they don't call him King Carl for nothing."

Dan, age 14

High school football team

High school track

High school band

4

I almost lost my little brother before I even knew him. I was almost seven the day my parents brought Tom home. He had just turned two. And to put it lightly, he was a crier. All night long he would wail these ear-piercing wails, shrill like a police whistle, and my parents didn't know what to do. It went on like that for months, and finally one day, they came into my room and told me they were going to take Tom back.

"What do you mean, take him back?" I asked.

"Back to the orphanage," my dad said.

I felt my stomach drop. "Why?"

"It's just better this way," my dad said.

Looking back, I'm not really sure why the news of Tom going back to the orphanage hit me so hard, as in reality, I barely knew the kid. But for whatever reason, I'd felt a very strong connection to Tom from the day my parents brought him home. I had big plans for us. We were going to be the best of friends, brothers banded together in a house full of girls, and as I watched my parents load him into the car and drive off for Portland, it felt like all of that hope was being taken away. I remember feeling extra lonely that night, but when I woke up the next morning, much to my surprise, Tom was sleeping soundly in his bed, not a tear to be found.

"We prayed on it the whole way," my dad said, "and we just couldn't do it. This is Tom's home. This is where he belongs. We're his family."

Every time I think about this day, it makes me happy.

So here we are, some eight years later, even closer than I thought we would be. We share a room and throw darts at our elephant wallpaper. We sneak looks at a stack of *Playboys* we found in the woods. We escape the chaos of the house by going fishing, waking up early to dig for worms, an ironic image of two adopted kids looking for peace on the Lost River. My mom tells me how much Tom looks up to me, how he wants to be just like me, and I guess I believe her.

Even though I can't really understand why.

As I head into the 10th grade at Henley High, I'm a small fish in a small pond—5'5" and 120 pounds, a mini afro as curly as a pig's tail, a JV scrub who gets picked on in the lunchroom. My best friend is a kid by the name of Don Sherman. We play trumpet in the marching band. I thought I had a girlfriend for a brief minute, but then her dad met me, realized I was black, and immediately forbade his daughter from seeing a "Negro."

It's these types of things that I sometimes think about telling the therapist, but I never actually do. Perhaps as a defense against some of the negative places my mind could go, I've become a profoundly positive person. I always look on the bright side. Always make the best of things. Because in the end, for lack of a better explanation, I just don't like to be sad. I don't like to talk sad. Think sad. Feel sad. So adamant am I in my defense against sadness that when the commercial for starving kids in Africa comes on, I literally get up and walk out of the room.

Plus, why would you complain about your life when it could be so much worse?

Before we moved to the farm, we lived down the street from a lady who took in foster kids on a temporary basis. They rode on my same bus to school, so I'd get to know their faces.

But I knew not to make friends with them because in a week or two, a month tops, they'd be gone, never to be seen or heard from again, off to some other foster home or back to their messed-up parents. The first time I picked up on this game of musical homes these kids were stuck in was the first time I really started to appreciate my family. I have a home to call my own. I have parents who love me. I have snowy Christmas mornings in a big warm house and a freezer full of steak. Like a lot of kids, I've got my insecurities. But unlike a lot of kids, I'm happy.

What makes me the happiest in the whole world is playing sports. To me, competition is the world's truest equalizer. Put two guys on a field or a track and it doesn't matter which one's black and which one's white, which one's adopted and which one isn't, which one's rich and which one's poor. I love the idea that the coolest kid in school can be humbled by the band geek, if the band geek happens to run like the wind.

Over the summer, my track coach, Larry Hunt, suggests I enter a local decathlon.

"I think you could do well," he says.

I've never even attempted most of the events in the decathlon, but I did pole vault as a freshman, which most people will tell you is the hardest one. I guess Coach Hunt thinks I can figure out the rest over the next two weeks.

"OK," I say. "What the heck."

So a few days later Coach Hunt and I head out to the track, where he introduces me to the shot put, the discus, the javelin and the hurdles. He teaches me the glide technique in the shot (which means you lunge forward rather than spin to create your momentum), and he offers me a few tips about the other throws. But he's mostly concerned about the hurdles, which, outside of the pole vault, is arguably the hardest event for a track athlete to pick up. First there is the obvious challenge of getting over 10 hurdles at top speed, and this is to say nothing of getting your steps right in between jumps.

Coach Hunt, who's about 6 foot 9, says to me, "OK, the way you want to do this is to take three steps in between hurdles. This way you jump off the same leg every time."

The three-step is not easy. And for the most part, it can't be taught. You're either fast enough, with a long enough stride and enough explosiveness to clear the hurdle from about seven feet out, or you're not. And the fact is, most people can't do it. Most people, good athletes even, need that fourth step, if not a fifth, and that's if they can even clear the hurdle at all—which explains the look on Coach Hunt's face after I've just three-stepped the entire way, without so much as touching a single hurdle, on my very first try.

"Wow," he says. "You just made that look a lot easier than it is."

Like I said—physically smart.

On the morning of the decathlon, which is being held at Henley, I'm feeling good. I know I'm inexperienced, but I'm pretty sure I'm going to run roughshod over these guys. I've become supremely, if not naïvely confident in my ability, or at least my speed, even if most people don't even know my name. I think to myself, *Just get me to the start line and let me go, and try not to choke on my dust.*

But it doesn't quite go down that way. I'm fast, which keeps me competitive, but I had no idea how hard this was going to be. This 10-events-in-two-days thing is for the birds. I score 5,583 points, good enough for fourth place, but I'm exhausted.

The math of a decathlon is pretty deceiving, as all told, over the course of a two-day competition, the amount of time that a decathlete is actually competing, actually running or jumping or throwing, is only about eight minutes. But it's the cumulative total of those days that gets you. It's like flying across the country with 10 layovers. Sure, most of that time you're sitting around, either in the terminal or on the airplane. But still, when it's all said and done, when you finally get to your destination and set your bags down and fall face first onto the bed, it feels as though you've just finished climbing Mt. Everest.

And then, just for fun, you have to get back up and run the 1500-meter.

I ask myself, Who in their right mind would ever want to be a decathlete? Who would willingly sign up for this kind of long, drawn-out punishment? I resolve that this will be my last decathlon. From now on, I'm a sprinter. A hurdler. A long jumper.

Heading into the 11th grade I've sprouted up some six inches, putting me right at six feet. I decide to quit my job washing dishes at Sambo's Diner and go out for the football team, and even though I haven't played since junior high on account of being too small, I manage to make the squad as a wide receiver. Coach says I'm raw. Undeveloped. But if I work hard, who knows, maybe I could be a player one day. I'm excited to see what I can do, but on the third day of practice, when I get hit so hard that my teeth rattle, I suddenly wonder whether I'm cut out for football. My passive, shy mentality is still one of a band geek. At halftime of one game, when the rest of the players head into the locker room, I stay on the field and do a trumpet solo in my shoulder pads.

I'll never forget my coach's response when I asked permission.

"You want to do *what*?"

You can imagine the confusion. I mean, high school trumpet players are supposed to sit in the stands and dream about playing football. But to have it be the other way around, to have the football player standing on the field thinking about playing the trumpet, well, it goes against all conventional high school wisdom. Fact is, if I were a star player, Coach never would've let me do it. But I'm just a backup. I wish I got to play more, but the guy in front of me, Steve Jones, is a total stud. Because of guys like him, we've made it to the state championship, and even if I'm just warming the bench, I can think of nothing cooler than being a part of a state championship team.

So of course, on the day of the game, I'm sick as a dog. Can't keep a bowl of chowder down. And now I'm sitting up in bed listening to the radio announcers going ape shit.

"Henley High! 1983 state champs!"

It's bad enough that I had to miss the game, but now, every day, I have to pass by the team picture in the school hallway—the picture that was taken the day of the game while I was at home dry heaving, the picture from which I'm conspicuously absent, the picture that serves as a daily reminder that to so many people, I don't even exist. I'm a band geek who happens to play sports. I offer glimpses of potential, scoring five touchdowns despite limited action, blocking 13 shots in a single basketball game, but for the most part I play to my personality, timid and unsure, like I'm trying not to piss anyone off. It's frustrating because I know there's a great athlete inside me, but for whatever reason, I just can't find a way to bring it out.

And then, one day it happens.

I'm at a track meet in the lush Illinois Valley, along the Rogue River, and somewhere in the middle of my first pass at the hurdles, everything clicks. I've been a good hurdler since that day 10 months ago when I first three-stepped, but this is the moment when it all falls in line. My stride pattern. My rhythm. Something has registered on an instinctual level, almost accidentally, like someone with a good singing voice suddenly hitting that one note they've never hit before. And when it happens, I take off like a bullet. Suddenly I'm running hard, even mean, with an aggression that belies my normally passive nature. I clear hurdle after hurdle, leaving the field in a trail of vapor, and by the end of the year I've hurdled all the way to a state title with a time of 14.84 seconds.

People ask, "Where did this O'Brien kid come from?"

I've burst onto the scene out of nowhere. One minute I'm a benchwarmer, the fast kid nobody knows about, and the next I'm a state champion. And as state champions will do, I head into my senior year walking just a little bit taller, with a little more swagger, high-fiving the fellas in the hallway. I've saved enough money from my string of odd summer jobs to buy a car, a shitty little Datsun that sounds like a windup toy, and for the first time in my life I have a real girlfriend. Laurie Walsh. She's a cheerleader. And the best part is, her father doesn't have a problem with his daughter dating a Negro.

When I walk out for my first day of senior football practice, I can tell that the guys are looking at me differently, perhaps because people tend to look at you the way you look at yourself.

With a year of experience and a whole new attitude under my belt, no longer am I just a fast runner. Now I'm a football player. Now I'm the guy rattling people's teeth. I'm confident. Aggressive. When I catch the ball on a quick slant, I'm no longer looking to avoid contact by dancing my way toward the sideline. I'm on the attack. And if you give even a peek of daylight, you can forget it. I'm gone.

By the end of the year, I'm averaging more than 26 yards per catch, and 10 of my 15 touchdowns have gone for 50 yards or more. I make first-team All-State. In our opening playoff game, after I take a reverse 70 yards for a touchdown, a man sitting next to my parents in the stands shouts, "Jesus! Them bucks sure can run!"

In Klamath Falls, bucks are synonymous with blacks.

I've always found it strange that people see me as black, as I've never really identified with that part of myself. In fact, to be perfectly honest, I actually feel a bit intimidated in the presence of black people—if not because I've never felt dark enough to be accepted as a "real" black, then simply because it's such a rare occasion. After all, Klamath Falls is 99 percent white. My friends are white. My parents are white. And if you hang around wolves long enough, no matter what color your coat is, pretty soon you start to feel like a wolf. Even if the other wolves see you as a buck.

We're playing Central High in the semifinals, and we have the home-field advantage. The night before the game it snows to a whiteout, and though we manage to get the field shoveled pretty well clean, it's still brutally freezing inside a thick layer of winter fog. I score two early touchdowns, but offense is hard to come by. We can't feel our fingers or toes, and when we talk in the huddle our breath looks like cigarette smoke. The pace of the game grinds to a halt, our legs a thousand pounds each, but after scraping and clawing for four quarters, we have the ball on Central's 1-yard line with two seconds left and the score tied 20-20.

Coach calls a timeout and jogs onto the field. We huddle up.

"What do you guys think?" he says. "Do we punch it in or go for the field goal?"

Under normal circumstances, kicking the field goal would be the obvious choice. But in high school football, on a night as cold as this one, field goals, even from the 1-yard line, are far from a guarantee. I know, because I'm the kicker. I've already kicked two extra points tonight, and they felt like my foot was colliding with a cinderblock.

Still, I'm confident. "Let me kick it, Coach. I'll make it."

Coach likes the confidence, and so it's settled. A field goal it is. All the guys start pumping me up, telling me I can do it. We break the huddle, and I take my normal three steps away from the holder. I take a deep breath, hold it, and give the nod that I'm ready. The ball is snapped. It's a good hold, but just as I go to kick it, the defensive end comes flying around the corner. He dives at my foot, and the ball never even makes it into the air. It's a clean block. The Central sideline erupts in celebration, and all I can do is stand there with my hands on my helmet.

You have to be shitting me. I just had a field goal from the 1-yard line blocked.

We never regain the momentum and end up losing in overtime, and when we hit the normal postgame hangout, Stagecoach Pizza, the mood is one of pure dejection. Guys are crying and hugging like somebody died, like the world is honestly coming to an end, but I told you: I don't do sad. When my dad sees me standing in the corner laughing and eating pizza with Don and Laurie, he can't help but be annoyed.

He says, "Geez, Danny. Aren't you even a little bit upset that you guys lost?"

I shrug my shoulders. "Why would I be upset? We had a great season."

This is one of the things about me that my dad has never been able to figure out, this perplexing contradiction of a kid who loves competition yet places such little emphasis on winning and losing. He sees me not throwing a tantrum and thinks I don't care, but to be clear, I think I probably care about winning just as much as the next guy. It's just that when it doesn't happen, I don't sit around crying about it. I forget it. Block it out. Look on the bright side. For if my life has taught me anything, it's that things rarely, if ever, go exactly the way you would've hoped.

5

Since my folks can't afford to pay one penny toward tuition, the only way I'm going to college is on a full-ride scholarship. I've known this for some time. But so far the only school to offer me anything, for either track or football, is little ole Oregon Tech—which is in Klamath Falls and does nothing for my ego, let alone my clichéd desire to get away from the only town I've ever known. For what it's worth, I have been on recruiting trips to both Oregon and Oregon State. Oregon offered to let me walk on, which means no money, while Oregon State offered me half.

But half doesn't cut it. I need a full boat. I told you, my parents don't have one dime. So right then and there I make a commitment to myself—a commitment to be all track, all the time. No distractions. I'll be a man on a mission. I even break up with my girlfriend as a show of my focus, and though I'm probably more upset than she is, I find a weird sort of strength in the sacrifice. Like I'm steeling myself. Proving something. It's a troubling sign of things to come: When I have a goal in mind, everything and everyone else gets pushed away. At my next few meets I run and jump pretty well, which leads to a call from Mike Keller, the head coach at the University of Idaho. He says he's going to be in Eugene for the NCAA Championships, and after the meet he'd like to drive down to Klamath and meet with my folks and me.

I've never even heard of the University of Idaho, but yeah, I guess that would be fine.

Keller doesn't look anything like he sounds. I don't know what I was expecting, but it wasn't a stout, Tom Skerritt look-alike with a Hollywood mustache and a thick head of salt-and-pepper hair. We go into the living room, and for the next few hours Coach Keller transforms into a used-car salesman. He's talking so slick and quickly that nobody can get a word in edgewise, leaving my parents and me to do nothing but look at each other in confusion. He says they have a Norwegian decathlete, Trund Knaplund, who just finished fourth in Eugene and is now coming back to coach next year.

"He's going to help you a lot."

But I don't want to be a decathlete.

"You're going to love it in Moscow."

Moscow? Isn't that in Russia?

"Actually," he continues, as though reading my mind, "Moscow's a lot like Klamath Falls. You're going to feel right at home."

The guy is an absolute salesman, a true master of the living room. He says everything in a way that would suggest I've already agreed to attend Idaho, like a telemarketer that says, "So, will you be donating 10 or 20 dollars today, sir?" before you've offered to donate anything. And his rebuttals are locked and loaded in the chamber, ready to fire at a moment's notice. I say I'd like to wait to sign until after the state meet, just in case I run really well and suddenly get a few more offers. He says most schools are done recruiting. I say I'd like some time to think about it. He says, "What's there to think about?"

"Have any other schools offered you a full scholarship, Dan?"

"No."

"And you *do* need a full scholarship to go to school, right?"

"Yes."

"So like I said, what's there to think about?"

He slides a letter of intent across the table and hands me a pen.

"That's an offer for a full scholarship. Tuition. Housing. Meals. Everything. I'm ready to commit to you right now, Dan. What do you say?"

I look to my parents, but all they do is scrunch their shoulders and turn their palms up like I've just asked for directions in a foreign language. They never went to college. They hesitate to advise me. My mom says, "It's your decision," but I can see it written all over her face that I would be an idiot to pass this up. To her, and I think to Coach Hunt and my dad, too, the situation is simple: I need money, this guy's offering it, what's the hold up? I can't argue with that logic. But I keep going back to the state meet in my head. What if I dominate? What if I win three or four titles or run some ridiculous time and suddenly USC or Washington comes calling? Then what?

Keller's eyes are locked on me. He's not leaving without a signature.

I take one last look around the room, breathing in the silence, and finally I settle on the two words that so often precede a piss-poor decision: Screw it. Idaho isn't Washington or Oregon, but it's not Oregon Tech, either. I sign the letter, and though I don't know it yet, tomorrow, when Coach Keller returns to campus, he will walk straight into his athletic director's office and tell him that he has just signed the greatest athlete in the history of the University of Idaho.

If signing with Idaho, at first, felt like a concession, like I was only doing it because of a lack of options, then I have to admit, it's feeling better by the day. Now I don't feel the pressure to land a scholarship. Now I don't feel like I absolutely have to win every event, though after I take first at the district meet in the 100m, 300m intermediate hurdles, high hurdles and long jump, Coach Hunt is pretty confident that I'm going to follow up that performance by sweeping all four events at the state meet. When the great Moses Malone was asked how he thought the 1983 playoffs were going to go for his Philadelphia 76ers, he responded, quite famously, by simply saying, "Fo, Fo, Fo," meaning he believed the Sixers were going to sweep through the three playoff series in four games each. Since I plan on sweeping four events at state, not three, we have come up with an adjusted saying around practice.

"Mark it down," we joke. "At state, Dan's going Fo, Fo, Fo, and just one Mo."

For me, this is all in good fun, but Coach Hunt decides to make the predictions public, telling a local newspaper reporter that I'm going to win four state titles and show the kids from Sutherlin that I'm the best. Sutherlin is a powerhouse track program in the northern part of the state. Their sprinters can really go. And when they get wind of Coach Hunt's brash prediction, they fire back in their own article by saying, essentially, "Who the heck is Dan O'Brien? If he's so good, why hasn't he been at any of the big meets?"

It's true, unfortunately, that I don't often run and jump against the guys from bigger schools. In fact, this is probably one of the reasons I wasn't recruited very hard. Coaches want to see you going against, and beating, the best competition, and going to a small school like Henley doesn't often afford me that opportunity. I did win the hurdles at a big invitational at Oregon State last year, and I am, of course, the reigning state champ. So if I really wanted to, I do have some ammunition to fire back at the Sutherlin guys. But I'm not much of a trash talker, especially not before a race. The way I figure it, talk is never cheaper than before a race. We'll all know who's fastest soon enough.

The state meet is taking place just outside Portland at Mt. Hood Community College, and it's pouring rain. Not exactly prime race conditions, but we're lucky to catch a brief window of blue sky for the 100-meter. I look down the start line and see Paul Villagran, one of the kids from Sutherlin, and for maybe the first time in my athletic life, I'm really, truly, nervous. I'm not sure if it's the pressure of living up to my coach's hype or the fact that my track shoes are being held together by dental floss, but either way, this is intense. No matter the level, everything stops for a 100-meter final. Every eye in the place is on that start line.

Set . . . Bang!

I get out of the blocks clean, as opposed to spinning my tires, and after 15 meters I'm running scared. Of what, I'm not entirely sure. But there's definitely fear in my heart. And it's making me fly. It's as though I'm weightless, while everyone else is dragging a grand piano. Fifty meters in and I'm no longer running just to win. I'm running to make a statement. I accelerate through the finish, throwing my hands in the air when I cross with a personal best time of 10.97 seconds—which is even more impressive given that it's an electronic race, as up until now everyone has stolen a few tenths from the stopwatch.

I have no idea how the Sutherlin kid finished, only that it wasn't anywhere near me. When I walk by him I don't say anything—because hey, I don't need to. To race is to erase all questions. A race is fair and final. There is no disputing that this is my day. My meet. In addition to my 100-meter win, I go on to validate my coach's prediction by winning the 110m high hurdles with a time of 14.65, the 300m intermediate hurdles in 39.42, and the long jump with a mark of just over 23 feet.

So dominant is my individual performance that I finish second in the team competition all by myself, without a single point being scored by one of my teammates. Think about that for a second. All these other teams are getting point contributions from multiple athletes, sometimes as many as six or seven, and I manage to finish a close second to Sutherlin High all by myself. Yeah, I'd say that's a statement. Especially for a kid whose shoes are falling apart. As I'm doing an interview with a local newspaper reporter, Coach Hunt walks past and winks.

"Fo, Fo, Fo," he says.

And just one Mo.

Even though I swore I would never do another decathlon, and despite my full intention to convince Coach Keller of my single-event potential upon my arrival in Moscow, after graduation, at the urging of Coach Hunt, I half-heartedly agree to compete in that same Southern Oregon Decathlon that I competed in during my 10th-grade summer—and I'll be damned if I don't end up qualifying for the Junior Olympics. Coach Hunt is ecstatic.

"Do you realize what an accomplishment this is?" he says.

"I guess so."

"You *guess so*? You qualified for the Junior Olympics in an event you've only tried twice in your life. Just think if you actually put in some work."

There's that word again. *Work*. To me, that's what the decathlon feels like. And even worse, it feels like thankless, unappreciated work. From where I'm sitting, nobody cares about the decathlon. Nobody lines up to watch a long, slow, 10-event grind the way they do a world-class 100-meter or long jump. In fact, the only person I've ever met who gives two shits about the decathlon is Coach Hunt, whose obsession ranks somewhere between nerdy and downright weird. For years he's been keeping track of marks and times and recording them like a human almanac, which is why he can tell you what a high school kid in Ohio scored last week as quickly as he can tell you his phone number. But his claim to fame is his supposed brush with Bruce Jenner.

The story always sounded strange to me, but Coach Hunt, apparently, was sitting close to the track at the '76 Olympics, and being the statistician he is, he was keeping a running total of all the decathlon scores. When Jenner crossed with a lightning-fast time of just under 4:12 in the 1500m, before the official scores had even been posted, Coach Hunt knew he'd broken the world record with 8,634 points.

"I whistled and yelled to him that he'd broken the world record," Coach Hunt gleams.

Personally, I doubt Jenner even heard or saw him in all that madness. But even if he did, I doubt even more that he needed anyone to tell him he'd broken the record. I'm sure he knew the exact time he needed to run. But oh, how Coach Hunt loves to tell that story. Decathletes are heroes to him. He tells me how he's studied the proud American tradition in this underappreciated event, comparing and contrasting the differing style of guys like Rafer Johnson and Bob Mathias and Bill Toomey.

Clearing Hurdles

But those names just don't mean anything to me.

I'd way rather be the next Carl Lewis.

Speaking of which, one of the coolest parts about the Junior Olympics is that they're being held at the L.A. Coliseum in conjunction with the 1984 Olympic trials, meaning I will be running on the same track as all the stars. And right now all the rage is about this Carl Lewis guy. He's only 22, and already he's recorded the second-best long jump and second-best 200m in history—28 feet, 3 inches and 19.75 seconds. Even more impressive was the 9.97 100m he ran to become the first guy to go under 10 seconds at low altitude. *Track and Field News*, the so-called bible of the sport, has named him its athlete of the year two years running, and now, with all the flair and charisma that has already come to define him, he says he's going to match the great Jesse Owens' legendary feat of winning four gold medals at this year's Olympics. His quest to do so begins this weekend, and I'll be there.

I might not be pumped about doing another decathlon, but that's pretty cool.

We're staying at my Aunt Kathy's house, and on the morning of my event, she sees me restitching my track shoes with fresh dental floss.

"You're not seriously going to run in those, are you?" she says.

"What do you mean? I won four state titles in these babies."

"I don't care what you won in them," she says. "I'm not letting you run in the Junior Olympics in those rags. What size are you?"

"It's fine, Aunt Kathy. Really."

Honestly, the shoes are no big deal. So they're starting to look like a baby tiger's chew toy. So what. I've gotten used to not having the best of things, and I'm plenty confident in my sewing talents. But Aunt Kathy won't have it.

"What size are you?" she insists.

"Eleven."

"OK, I'll be right back."

She grabs her keys and runs out the door, and 20 minutes later she returns with a brand-new pair of Nikes. They're snazzy, fluorescent green with a bright orange swoosh, but they're stiff as a board. Just before my 100-meter, I think about switching them out for my old pair, but I don't, and perhaps as a consequence I fail to break 11 seconds in the 100m and barely long jump 22 feet. It leads to a disappointing first day, but really, it's hard to be upset. Not only am I looking around in awe of this giant stadium, but now I'm standing trackside as Carl Lewis goes whizzing past in the 100m prelim. All I can think is, *Holy shit, this guy's fast.* I mean, I knew he was fast. Of course. But to see it from this close, to actually *feel* him rush past, it honestly defies words. This dude is from another planet.

My second day of competition goes much better. For starters, I spot Marcus Allen and get his autograph. I also establish personal bests in the discus, pole vault and javelin. And for the first time in my life, I run a sub-five-minute 1500m, crossing in a time of 4:57.64. By the end of the day I've climbed all the way up to fourth place—which is even better when you consider that the three guys who finished ahead of me are all college guys.

Coach Hunt is almost giddy. "You scored better than Kip Janvrin," he says.

Kip Janvrin, from Iowa, is the premier high school decathlete in the country. And somehow I beat him, meaning I will finish the year as the No. 1-ranked decathlete in the country. Can you believe that? This is only the third decathlon I've done in my whole life, and I'm No. 1 in the United States.

"I'm proud of you, Danny," my dad says. "Real proud."

My dad tells me this all the time. He's my biggest fan. And yet, I don't yearn for his approval in the way a lot of boys do their fathers. To me, my dad's just another buddy. A pal. I think he wants it to be more. I think he wants us to have that classic, All-American relationship. But as the years have passed, I've just never fully engaged in my half of the deal. I've only let the connection go so far. I think it's easy to blame the biology, or lack thereof, but even if I wasn't adopted, even if I was born into the picket-fence family, I think to some degree I'm just wired to be a bit of a lone soul.

Even my mom will tell you that I tend to exist in my own world a lot. At school I sit in the back of class and stare out the window, my mind running off to places far beyond the hills of Klamath Falls. For as long as I can possibly remember, I've always felt that there was something more out there for me, that this life I'm living is merely a stopover until I get to where I'm going. Growing up in Klamath has been great. The big family, the farm, the Friday night football games—all great. But like I said, I just know there's something more out there for me. And I can't wait to find out what it is.

The day I get back to Klamath feels like the first day of the rest of my life. It's time to go. Time to fly the coup. In fact, I can't even wait for the end of summer to get out of the house. A guy I know, Dave Simpson, has an apartment in town, and he says I can crash on his couch until I leave for school if I give him a few hundred bucks a month. I make rent by working at Abby's Pizza and the local carwash.

Toward the end of the summer, Carl Lewis wins his four gold medals.

"Dude, I stood 10 feet from him," I proudly tell Don, to which he responds by saying, "maybe someday Carl Lewis will say he stood 10 feet from you."

I end up selling my car to a girl for $400, which is every cent I have to my name on the day I leave for college. Don's enrolled at Oregon State, but he's going to drive me the eight hours to Moscow before heading to Corvallis. I've got two suitcases. That's it. I go back to the farm to say goodbye, and my mom gives me a quick hug and says, "Be good." My dad doesn't say a whole lot more. I peek into the other room and wave goodbye to a few of my sisters, who hardly look up from what they're doing.

"Have fun," Sara says.

I guess when you withdraw, you can't expect others not to do the same.

So there is no traditional send-off. No tears. No last words of wisdom. No standing in the driveway waving. I simply toss my suitcases in Don's car and we burn out, and the moment we hit the highway, excitement fills the air.

"College, baby! Here we come!"

With the windows rolled down and the radio turned up, it feels as though we're inside a movie scene—two kids at the start of a journey. The road is open and the sky is big, and as the green, quietly rolling hills go whizzing past, my old life fading to a blur, I turn over my shoulder to take one last look at everything I'm leaving behind.

Now, if only I could've seen the trouble that lay ahead.

DAN CROSSES THE VICTORY LINE

100-yard dash, 10.84 seconds   *Danny O'Brien*

Hurdle warm-up

Shot Put

One of my biggest pet peeves in all of sports is watching a baseball pitcher try to hit. To watch them walk up to the plate like a limp noodle, already defeated, no expectations, waving that bat around with absolutely no intention of using it, is embarrassing. If you want to be a hitter, then be a friggin' hitter. Think like a hitter. Act like a hitter. Become a hitter in your head. Become Mike Schmidt. George Brett. Mickey fuckin' Mantle. Put on a pair of grimy batting gloves and stand up there with some conviction. Dig in. Stare down the barrel and see yourself pounding the shit out of that ball.

As the great Milt Campbell once told me, "Half of being is believing."

At 6'2" and 190 pounds, I'm a sprinter. A jumper. I'm not a shot-putter. But when it's time to throw, I become one. I return my mind to the Idaho weight room, iron plates banging off the floor, heavy-metal music blaring. I get a nasty snarl on my face, banging my hands together hard, chalk flying in the air as I stomp toward the ring to the tune of Metallica's "Enter Sandman."

"Sleep with one eye open . . . Gripping your pillow tight . . ."

It is the fall of 1992. I'm in France for the DecaStar Invitational, and I've publicly announced that I'm here to break the world record. The fans are rowdy and festive, as is almost always the case overseas. They begin with a loud, rhythmic clap as I make my way into the ring, and I play to it, urging them to get louder, louder, and they oblige, cheering raucously, the energy building to a crescendo. In other events you can get yourself into trouble by trying to ride the crowd, losing your technique in the emotion, but the shot put is about pure power and explosion, and adrenaline goes a hell of a long way toward both.

I whisper to myself, "Turn it loose."

I push out of the back, hit my power position, turning my hips with everything I've got and release, screaming as the 16-pound shot leaves my fingertips. Like a hitter who knows he just jacked one out of the park, I know it's big. I don't even watch it land. I just throw my arms in the air and turn to the crowd and roar, and they go wild. I turn back to check the mark—54 feet, 8 inches.

Pound for pound, it will go down as the single greatest shot put in history.

6

Sitting just eight miles east of the Washington border on an expanse of green, rolling hills, Coach Keller was right: Moscow looks a lot like Klamath Falls. But that doesn't make me feel any closer to home. I remember thinking that Moscow was in Russia, and as Don and I pull onto campus, that's about as far away as I feel.

I step out from the car and gaze out over the bustling campus.

"So, what now?" Don says.

"I have no idea."

And I'm not just saying that for effect. I literally have no idea. I don't know where I'm supposed to go, who I'm supposed to see, what I'm supposed to do. Nobody has told me anything. Not Coach Keller. Not my parents. Everywhere I look I see families—moms and dads carrying boxes, helping their kids get settled, and here I am completely lost, alone, two suitcases in hand like a runaway at the train station.

At the housing building, there's a line that snakes around the corner. I wait an hour just to find out that I haven't filled out the paperwork that was apparently sent in the mail. When I finally make it to my dorm room, I meet my new roommate, Nolan Harper, who's as big as a house and has the personality of a coiled rattlesnake. He takes one look at my suitcases and says, "Oh hell no. I don't need me no fucking roommate, man."

Say no more.

I go straight back to the resident advisor, Scott, and beg him for a different room. He chuckles, making me think he might know Nolan, and hands me a new key.

"Second floor."

Still, all I see are families, moms unpacking, situating, dads on their hands and knees putting furniture together. I push in the door to my new room to find a desk, a couch, and a set of bunk beds as bare as the bone-white walls.

Don says, "I hope you packed some bed sheets."

Shit.

Don laughs. "Don't worry, man, we can get some at K-Mart."

Problem is, K-Mart doesn't have bed sheets—only sleeping bags, which cost 25 bucks each. Throw in a pillow, a case of Olympia beer, a pepperoni pizza for dinner, and the paperwork fee I had to pay at the housing office, and my $400 is flying out of my pocket like I'm at a Vegas slot machine. At this rate I'm going to be busted by the end of the weekend.

"Come on, man, let's have a beer," Don says, trying to cheer me up, and in no time at all, we're hammered.

Over the next four years, drinking will be my solution to a lot of things.

The newly constructed Kibbie Dome is the signature landmark of the Idaho campus—a state-of-the-art facility with a retractable turf football field, 300 meters of indoor track surface and an artificial glow that paints the walls with a lime tint. Keller is insistent that I'm a decathlete, but I've got other plans. I think I can be a sprinter or a hurdler, or even a long jumper. I'm eager to prove myself against a trio of Jamaican sprinters— Dave Smith, Everton Wanliss and Chris Stokes, all of whom have low-10-second speed. On the very first day of practice, when we're running what is supposed to be a leisurely, five-mile jog around the Idaho golf course, I go right to the front and kick through the finish like I'm in the Olympics. And I've been going full throttle ever since.

"Yo, Fresh," Everton often says in his thick Jamaican accent. "Chill out, mon."

Everton's not worried that I'm perhaps showing him up, that I outkicked him and everyone else in a 200-meter run inside the dome last week. He's just trying to help me. He doesn't believe in going this hard this early in the season. They do things differently in Jamaica. Whereas American coaches sometimes have a reputation for overusing their top sprinters, like a horse trainer who can't resist the urge to run a good thoroughbred into the ground, Jamaicans typically train to the age-old mantra of quality over quantity, saving their legs for race time, money time.

If Everton and the boys had it their way, at least during the fall, they'd be running half as much and half as hard. Personally, I'd be fine with the half as much part. But the half as hard part? I wouldn't even know how to do that. As you go through the world of track, you discover that there are two kinds of athletes: racers and runners. I'm a racer. I don't care if we're in a parking lot, if you line me up next to someone, I only know one way to go, and it just so happens to be the same way I party.

All out.

The party scene on campus is something of a political situation. It's all about who you know. Every frat has a guest list for its parties, and the goal of every weekend is to get on one of those lists. But it's not easy. Fraternity guys don't want a bunch of dudes screwing up the all-important girl-to-guy ratio. They even use these cheap hand stamps as a way of keeping order at the door, picking and choosing who they want to let in with a fine-tooth comb, turning most everyone away with the annoying power of a Studio 54 bouncer.

Lucky for me, my new roommate, Greg Bowen, knows a lot of the guys in the Sigma Nu frat, so we've pretty much got an open invite. Of all the people I've met, Greg's about the only guy who parties as hard as me. Together we're a wrecking crew. We'll dust a fifth of the nastiest tequila on earth before we even leave our dorm, and the moment we walk into the party, already wasted, people will yell, "Quick! Somebody hide the keg!" I take a dangerous amount of pride in the fact that I can party with the best of them.

And so the routine goes. Football games. Frat parties. The college scene has sucked me in like a tractor beam. One night we're drinking suicide juice, a giant washtub of straight vodka with floating fruit slices, and the next thing I know I'm hanging over my railing puking so hard that my feet are lifting off the ground. The next morning I hear a banging on my door. It's Mitch Wolf, a big, bearded pole-vaulter who looks like he did hard time or rode with Hell's Angels, or perhaps both. And he's pissed.

"You puked on my porch last night."

"Oh shit," I laugh. "Sorry, Mitch. We were drinking suicide juice."

"I don't care what you were drinking. Just get your ass down there and clean it up."

Mitch isn't the kind of guy you say no to, so now I'm walking downstairs with a wet towel. A few minutes later I'm on my hands and knees scrubbing up my own vomit like fucking Cinderella. And somewhere in the middle of it all, it occurs to me that maybe, just maybe, I ought to tone down the partying. I know college is supposed to be fun and all, but maybe a guy who's always having fun is a guy who isn't getting very much done.

When I do actually make it to class, I'm hung over as shit. I sit in the very back of giant lecture halls and completely zone out. And by the end of the semester, it's caught up with me.

"I got your grades," Coach Keller says.

"And?" As if I don't know what he's going to say.

"They're not good."

"Economics?"

"So you know."

"I had a feeling. That class is more boring than a game of chess."

"Well, boring or not, an F is an F. And you don't have anything other than C's in your other classes."

NCAA regulations dictate that all athletes must maintain at least a 2.0 GPA in order to be deemed academically eligible. With three C's and an F, I'm coming in at a paltry 1.5.

"But it's actually not as bad as it sounds," Keller continues. "We were probably going to redshirt you, anyway."

With how well I've been doing in practice, I'm kind of shocked to hear this. But in a way, it's a relief. Now I don't feel like such a colossal screw-up. Now, when I go home for Christmas break and everyone's asking if I'm going to have any meets in Oregon so maybe they can come watch me run, I can tell them that I'm redshirting because our team is loaded with Jamaican sprinters, and even more so, because Coach wants me to save a year of eligibility so I can dominate even more when I'm a senior—which is so much better than having to tell them I tanked economics.

It's the beginning of my lies to not only my friends and my family, but to myself.

Back in Klamath, there seems to be a lot of tension in the house. My parents, though I don't know it, are on their way to a divorce. One of my sisters has dropped out of school. And my little brother is at obvious odds with my dad. Growing up, Tom idolized my dad even more than he did me. He longed for his approval in a way that I never did, and now that he's in high school and trying to carve out his own athletic identity, I have a feeling my dad, even if he doesn't realize it, is constantly comparing him to me. Tom's becoming a good little athlete in his own right. He can squat damn near 400 pounds, and he's a bull on the wrestling mat. But to compare him to me wouldn't be fair. We were born different. One day my dad's talking about Tom and how hard he works, and I wish Tom could be there to hear it—right up until the last thing he says.

"I'm telling you, Danny," he says. "If we could just put Tom's heart in your body, we would have the greatest athlete in the world."

He means this as a compliment to Tom, but I know Tom wouldn't take it that way.

I took the bus home from Idaho, having to borrow 20 bucks from the father of a girl who gave me a ride as far as Salem. But my mom has offered to take me back. On the way out of town she says to me, "So, there's something I've been wanting to tell you."

"What's that?"

"Well, it's probably nothing, but a few months ago, at your state track meet, there was a man in the stands."

"A man?"

"From what I could tell, he was all by himself. He didn't seem like he was connected with any of the schools or runners. He looked to be about 40, give or take, and he was just sitting there watching your races."

She pauses, thinking about what she wants to say, and how she wants to say it.

"And?" I probe.

"And . . . well . . . he looked a lot like you."

"Like *me*?"

She nods, and I immediately put two and two together. The state meet was just outside Portland. I was born *in* Portland. My parents were said to be of college age or thereabouts when I was born, which would make them somewhere around 40 now. I feel my stomach sink when I consider the implication. Could it be? Is it possible that the man in the stands, as crazy as it sounds, was my father? And if it was, was that the first time he'd come to watch me? Is it possible that he's been watching from afar all along? Reading the newspaper with pride? Checking in on me from time to time just to make sure I'm OK?

Does my father know who I am, when I have no idea who he is?

"I hope I didn't upset you," my mom says. "I just thought you might like to know."

I honestly don't even know what to say, and it's times like these that my ability to block things out comes in handy. Before we've even arrived in Moscow, I've already forgotten this entire conversation. I don't want to think about the father I've never met. I've never wanted to. I don't see the point. When I get back to school, I immerse myself in track and the party scene. I keep my mind busy.

I'm still working out with the team, and as a decathlete, I'm a freelancer at practice. I spend some time with the sprinters and jumpers, then even more with the throwers. To be in the weight room with a bunch of shot-putters and discus guys is something of a primal experience. Heavy metal music blaring. Chalk flying in the air. These guys are huge, and the weight they're throwing around is absurd—500 on the bench, 700 on the squat rack, iron bars literally bending in the shape of a rainbow. To get themselves pumped for a lift, these guys will spit and scream and honest-to-God slap each other in the face.

"Come on, you pussy!"

"One time, baby!"

"One, two, three . . . aaaaahhhhhh!"

From the outside listening in, with all the raw, testosterone-filled grunts reverberating around that room, you'd think a band of gorillas were mating, and for a skinny sprinter like me, that can be intimidating. But once you inject yourself into the middle of it, once you make the commitment and forget your inhibitions and start throwing around a few of your own grunts, you start to lose yourself in the intensity. Tim Taylor is a badass discus thrower, and he has sort of taken me under his wing. Sometimes we go out to the field on Saturdays, where Tim is beginning to school me in the art of discus mechanics.

"30,000 throws a year," Tim says. "That's what it takes."

John Powell, a three-time Olympian, is considered the grandfather of American discus throwers. He competed in the '70s, and he was famous for his belief that to be a real threat on the discus scene, a guy had to take 30,000 throws a year, which equates to about 100 throws every day. It's a ton of throws, no question. But that's the commitment of these single-event guys. This is all they do. A decathlete, on the other hand, has to find balance, sometimes to the point of spreading himself thin. After 20 or 30 throws I have to move on to something else, to the long jump or shot put or the monotonous drills Keller has me doing to improve my running form—which, by the way, are apparently working.

One day I run a 500-yard sprint with a guy by the name of Sam Koduah. Sam's from Ghana, and he can really go, but I pretty much match him stride for stride. When Sam crosses the line a shoe-length ahead of me, Keller looks at his stopwatch. A minute flat.

"Wow," he says. "You guys just finished a 10th of a second off the world record."

Yes sir, them bucks sure can run.

7

The legal drinking age in Idaho is 19, so now the bars are in play. Sometimes we hit a dive joint called the Corner Club, where there's a nail that hangs on a wooden beam some 11 feet off the ground—11 feet, 6 inches, to be exact. Legend has it that the nail was hung to commemorate NBA legend Gus Johnson, who played his college ball at Idaho and is said to have once jumped up and touched the indicated spot from a standing start. If he did, I consider that to be one of the great athletic feats of all time.

I mean seriously, 11-and-a-half feet from a standing start? That's crazy.

Even the great Bill Walton, who's almost seven feet before his feet leave the ground, is said to have come up woefully short of that nail. Virtually everyone who has ever stepped foot inside the Corner Club has tried and failed, and I'm no different. Every time I go in that place, after I slug a few beers and gather everyone around, making a total spectacle of myself, I start placing bets, reveling in the attention as the whole bar turns to watch. I never get close to the nail, but that's not the point. It's all about the attempt, the show, the spotlight. I'm the life of the party when I'm hammered. I'm loose and relaxed, not so worried about fitting in—which, of course, makes it that much easier to fit in. I high-five the fellas after I slam a shot of whiskey. I tell loud stories. I laugh. I dance. And then, at the end of almost every night, I run. It's a pretty odd thing, but that's what I do. I just get up and go, boom, just like that, don't tell anyone I'm leaving or anything, and nobody will see me for the rest of the night. It's a big joke with all my friends.

"Why are you always running from shit?" they laugh.

It's a better question than they think.

I think back to the way I used to leave the room when the starving kids commercial came on, the way I always avoided talking to the family counselor, the way I never wanted to address any of the things I might be struggling with for fear of starting down the slippery slope of sadness. All my life I've tried to paint the world rosy red, and here I am, still trying.

Every day Coach Keller asks me, "Everything OK, O'Brien?"

And every day I tell him, "Everything's fine, Coach. Just fine."

But everything's not fine. My grades, again, are shit, and my drinking is an issue. It's easy for a college kid to pass off his blackout binges as a phase, but there's a fine line between a college drinker and a legitimate alcoholic, and for me, that line is starting to get awfully blurry. At the end of the semester, I'm once again ineligible.

"That's it," Keller says. "You're going to lose your scholarship."

"Lose my scholarship? But how am I going to pay for school or housing?"

Keller snickers. "Maybe you should've thought about that before you decided not to go to class."

What can I say to that?

"You'll need to apply for grants," he says, "and hopefully get some financial aid."

"How do I do that?"

"I'll help you put together the applications. And I'll see about getting you some work this summer."

I get on with the university's physical plant. We do shit work like standing in a foot of nasty brown water while weed-eating the banks of a canal that runs the length of campus. I make 200 bucks a week and pick up the worst case of athlete's foot you've ever seen. A guy on the track team, Steve Krackenburg, is letting me crash at his pad. It's a shithole, with half a pole-vault pit in the living room as an extra bed. But I'm trying to save money.

I've stored some of my stuff in alumni housing, and at the end of the summer I need to get it out. An old guy named Duane, who's in charge of maintenance, gives me his key.

"Get your things," he says, "and be sure to bring the key back on Monday."

So I get my things and go back to my new dorm, and over the weekend, as I'm having a few beers and smoking a little weed, I start to wonder if this key that Duane gave me is, in fact, the master key to the whole campus. I don't know why it matters. It's not like I'm planning on breaking into the science lab or anything. I'm just curious. I decide to try it out on the storage closet in the hallway.

It's a bad idea.

I haven't even gotten the key in the lock before a resident advisor with a total hard-on for his job comes walking around the corner.

"Hey!" he barks. "What are you doing?"

I can tell right away this dude's on a power trip. I tell him it's no big deal, that I was just screwing around, that Duane lent me the key and that I'll return it on Monday. But he doesn't believe me. Says he thinks I stole the key. And the next thing I know I've got two cops knocking on my door. No bullshit. Cops. For *almost* opening a closet full of toilet paper.

"We're going to need you to come down to the station and give a statement."

So I do. I tell them exactly what happened, that Duane gave me the key and told me to return it Monday. But now Duane is changing his story. He's saying that he never gave me the key. He's saying he doesn't know how I got the key, basically implying that I stole it, because if he admits he gave it to me he's going to lose his job. It's my word against his, and predictably, I lose. I get charged with stealing university property, and though I get off with just 20 hours of community service, the damage has been done. Now Judge Hamlet knows who I am. He has an eye out for me. And it won't be long before we meet again.

It's the fall of 1986, the start of my third year in Idaho. I tell myself: *This is the year I get my shit straight. This is the year I turn it around and finally make good on all my potential.* In October, I watch Bill Buckner boot a routine grounder in the World Series and have no idea that a similar fate awaits me, that one day soon I will pull one of the most infamous screw-ups in sports history. I move into a new dorm, get a meal plan, and enroll in classes, but with my scholarship gone I can't foot any of the bills.

I've applied for the Pell Grant, but I'm getting declined. I can't figure out why. I know kids who are still getting monthly checks from their parents who've qualified. Finally, I call to see what the hell's happening.

A woman tells me, "It looks like your father's claiming you."

Lady, I'm adopted. You might want to clarify.

"On his taxes," she says. "He's claiming you as a dependent."

You have to be shitting me. I haven't seen a single penny from my parents since I was 16, and now my dad's claiming me as a dependent? Is that even legal? I call him up and ask him, beg him, to take me off his forms.

"Well hell," he jokes, "I deserve *something* for raising you guys, don't I?"

This is my dad. Never one to take things seriously. I remember one time, when I was probably seven or eight, my mom came into the kitchen saying she was worried about the bills. My dad started tickling me and making me laugh, saying, "Good, that means Danny and I don't have to!" He's a big kid, and that's fine. But I need this grant. It's probably my last chance to stay in school and get back on the team that I've never really been on in the first place.

"Just take me off, Dad," I say. "Please."

I never find out if he does, but a month later, when I still haven't qualified for the Pell Grant, I can only assume that he didn't, or couldn't. Either way, I'm screwed. All told, after a semester's worth of unpaid tuition and housing and meal-plan bills, I've racked up just under five grand in debt to the university. Forget getting back on the team or back in school—at this point, I'm just trying to keep a roof over my head. How long can I skate by living in the dorms without paying? I get a minimum-wage job selling protein powder at GNC with the intention of paying down my bill a little at a time, but the school

Clearing Hurdles

has turned the case over to a collection agency. I ignore phone calls almost every day. I know it's only a matter of time before they chuck me out on my ass.

Finally, it happens. I come home to three large men waiting outside my dorm.

"Pack your shit, my man," one guy says. "You've got 10 minutes."

If it's any consolation, they at least offer to drive me to wherever I'm going to sleep that night, which might be a park bench for all I know. I tell them no thanks. I can take care of myself. So there I am, standing outside my dorm, literally the same way I showed up three years ago—with two suitcases in hand and absolutely no fucking idea what to do. I eventually have to swallow my pride, walk to Greg Bowen's house, and ask him if I can crash on his couch for a while.

"Sure, man," he says. "What's wrong?"

Jesus, where do I start?

It's amazing how quickly things can get away from you. It seems like yesterday that Keller was sitting in my living room offering me the scholarship nobody else was willing to offer. I was supposed to be the best athlete in Idaho history, and three years later I've never even worn a fucking uniform. I still lie awake at night imagining myself running and winning in front of big, cheering crowds, but the last track meet I actually competed in was the Junior Olympics when I was 17 years old. I'm 21 now, and I'm in danger of pissing my entire life away. If I haven't already. The dreamer in me is a caged bird.

The hardest thing of all is to see everyone around me doing productive things. You know, going to school and stuff. Holding down jobs. Playing on the golf team. When I'm not behind the counter at GNC, I have nothing to do, nowhere to be. I feel worthless, but I don't know how to ask for help.

Sometimes I go into the Kibbie Dome and watch track practice from way up high in the stands. I'd give anything to be able to rewind my life three years and start over, to go back in time and do everything differently. But I can't. And the reality of that feels paralyzing,

I'm in a hole from which there seems no escape, so I drink to forget. Every night I go looking for parties, hitting the bars by myself, and if there is one certainty in life, it's this: nobody up to any kind of good can be found partying in the bars on a Tuesday night.

I start running with some local grunge-band guys, and before long the drinking turns into drugs. I've been smoking weed every day for a while, but now it's slipping into cocaine. That numbs me up real nice. One night we eat a bag of mushrooms, and when they kick in, when I go to the bathroom and look in the mirror, I literally don't recognize myself. My face is warped, melting. I look straight into the mirror and say, in complete confusion, "I have no idea who that person is."

The truth of a trip.

If you're feeling like this is never going to stop, like this is just one story after another of me doing stupid shit, welcome to my life. Momentum is a powerful thing, especially bad momentum, the proverbial snowball picking up speed. I just can't make any progress.

I pick up a second job officiating city league basketball games at night, and I even trade in my GNC gig for two bucks an hour more sanding wood cabinets on an assembly line. But every dollar I make goes straight to the school. I can't give Greg any money for rent. Hell, I can hardly buy food, though I always find a way to get beer.

I start writing bad checks around town, and before long, my P.O. box begins filling up with a whole new wave of collection notices. I wonder if there's a person in the world that I don't owe. I owe the university. I owe local businesses. I owe Greg and his roommates. I owe Keller the biggest apology in history. And when the bill, or at least one of the bills, finally comes due, when I get a notice to appear in court for the bad checks, I once again find myself standing before the honorable Judge Hamlet.

"Haven't we seen each other before?" he says.

"Yes, sir."

"Didn't I tell you to stay out of trouble?"

"Yes, sir."

"Well I'll tell you what, with the court fee, you owe $412. Can you pay that today?"

"No, sir."

"Can you come up with the money at all?"

"Maybe."

Hamlet gives me a few days to come up with the funds, and with nowhere else to turn, I reach out to my parents. My dad wishes he could help, but he doesn't have the money. I'm sunk. The next week I'm back in court telling Judge Hamlet that I won't be able to make good, and as I wait for my punishment, he instead asks me why I did it. Why am I writing bad checks all over town. I've become a pretty good liar over the years, but in this moment, I can only tell the truth.

"I don't know. I don't know why I do a lot of things."

He sentences me to four days in jail, saying I can serve them anytime in the next three months. Sadly, I don't have shit to do for the next four days. Let's get this over with.

"Sure thing," he says. "Bailiff."

They lead me into the county jail, strip me down and throw me in a blue jumpsuit with a number on the chest, and now I'm literally a caged bird. The first night the clock moves like molasses, second after agonizing second, something restless stirring in my stomach. As I lie awake on a concrete mattress next to a metal toilet, I can't stop thinking about all the people I've let down. All the promises I've broken. All the potential I've wasted. Somewhere along the way it occurs to me that this is the first time I've slept in an actual bed in almost a month. When jail is an upgrade, you know you're in the shitter.

In a moment of dark panic, I resolve to turn things around the very second I get out of this hellhole. No more drinking. No more smoking. I'm going to find a way to get back into school and back on the team. I've made these promises before, but this time I mean it. No more screwing around.

So what do I do the minute I get out?

I run to a buddy's house, load up a bong, and get high as a kite.

I don't know what the fuck I'm doing, but I feel powerless to stop it, the entire task of digging out of this huge hole seeming too daunting to even take the first step. So I just let it get worse. And worse. By the time Christmas rolls around, I'm too ashamed to even go home. I can't face my family. My friends. I tell them I have to work, which is a lie, as I've just been laid off from the cabinet shop. I spend Christmas morning alone, in Greg's big, empty house, eating cold macaroni and cheese and

Clearing Hurdles

drinking Keystone Light. I think about my family and how much I used to love the holidays, the way the snow would fall outside the window, the way the crackling fire would burn warm, the way Karen and I would sleep in the living room, in the sleeping bags my mom made for us, waiting for Santa. I miss my family. I never thought I would say that, but I do.

I never thought I would cry on Christmas.

High Jump

When I was 17 I went on a recruiting trip to Oregon State. The campus was old and quaint, like the town of Corvallis itself, the trees blossoming with spring color, and just off the backside of the track was an old shed. I'd first noticed it a year earlier when I was running in a big invitational, and now it was catching my eye again. I asked Coach McNeil what it was.

"You ever heard of Dick Fosbury?" he asked me.

I had to think for a second, but then it hit me. Dick Fosbury is the guy who reinvented the high jump. Forever jumpers had employed what was known as the straddle technique, meaning you go at the bar with a sort of head-first dive, pulling each leg over separately, like a hurdler only with your body parallel to the ground. It's hard to put into words, but basically you end up rolling over the bar to create the momentum to bring that back leg up, and Fosbury thought it to be a dated, even inefficient and difficult way of jumping. He thought he could go over much easier and make higher marks by going over backward. He put this new technique into play at the 1968 Olympics in Mexico City, where he broke the Olympic record and won the gold medal with a jump of 2.24 meters, which is just shy of 7 feet, 5 inches. They called it the "Fosbury Flop."

"Sure I've heard of Dick Fosbury," I told Coach McNeil. "Why?"

"Well, that shed is where he perfected his technique."

"You mean, Dick Fosbury went to Oregon State?"

Coach nodded. Smiled. "NCAA champion in '68-'69."

This blew my mind. The Fosbury Flop is famous, and the guy who invented it went to school right here. I looked at the shed and imagined a young, aspiring athlete all by himself. I saw him going over the bar time and again, tinkering with an idea. He was onto something. Right there, in that tiny shed, history was being made. An event was being revolutionized, changed forever, the bar literally being raised.

I don't know it yet, but one day people will say I did the same thing for the decathlon.

At Idaho with Mike Keller

8

It is February of 1988, and I'm about to hit rock bottom.

I've been combing the want ads for jobs, but the only thing I can find is a dishwashing position at Skippers. My first day is a Tuesday, and the sky is brewing. A storm is on the horizon. I hop on my bike and ride to the restaurant, bitter and cold, unable to believe that this is what my life has come to. I park my bike in the rack, and then, just as I'm about to walk inside, I see a man through the window, probably in his early 30s. He's waiting tables, and he stops me dead in my tracks. I watch him carrying plates and writing down orders, and as I do, I find myself wondering what he used to dream about. I can't imagine it had anything to do with Skippers. Surely there was a time when he wanted something more, perhaps even a time when he was on his way. But something happened, he fell off track, and now here he is. Life happens fast.

I look down at my watch. In two minutes, I'll be late for my first day of work.

I look back up at this waiter, and suddenly his face turns into mine. I am him. He is me. I see myself five years from now, 10 years from now, washing dishes at Skippers on a Tuesday, just another day in a life that could've been. When it starts to rain, I take it for a sign. I need this job, surely, but I suddenly have the strangest feeling that if I walk into that restaurant, I might never come out. The thought shakes me to my core. I can't do it. I can't go in.

If this is the point of no return, I can't cross it.

In a snap, panicked decision, I hop on my bike and head straight for Keller's house. As the rain sprays against my face, I'm planning a thousand speeches in my head. I pedal faster, my heart racing, and when I finally get there, when I drop my bike at the curb and walk up to his porch and softly ring the doorbell, I am literally shaking—and it has little to do with the rain. I have never been more desperate in all my life.

"O'Brien?" Keller says when he opens the door. "What the hell's the matter?"

I lay it all on the line.

"Coach, please. I need help. I know I'm better than this."

"I know you're better than this, too, Dan."

"So give me one more chance."

"I don't have any chances to give. You're out of chances."

"Please, Coach. I'm begging you. I swear I won't let you down again."

He has absolutely no reason to trust me, but he can hear the desperation in my voice, see it on my face. He takes in a deep breath and sighs it out, runs his hand through his thick hair. This goes against his better judgment.

"Come inside," he says. "I'm not making any promises, but let's see what we can do."

For all the bad decisions I've made in my life, I have a feeling that blowing off my first day at a brand-new job is going to end up being one of my best.

Three days after my desperate visit to Keller, he calls me up.

"Pack your bags," he says. "You're going to Spokane."

I don't even bother to ask questions.

"I'll be ready in an hour."

The plan is for me to spend the next few months in Spokane, Washington, which sits about 70 miles west of Moscow. I'll be going to Spokane Community College, where I'll have a chance to not only run on the track team (at the junior college level I have a clean eligibility slate), but also to retake the classes I've failed and raise my GPA to a level which will allow me to return to Idaho next fall. SCC operates on the quarter system. School has just started. On the ride there, Keller doesn't mention anything about this being my last chance. He doesn't have to.

The head track coach at Spokane Community is a guy by the name of Duane Hartman, and I can tell right away that he's as genuine as they come. When Keller and I walk into his office, he stands right up and shakes my hand.

"Hello, Dan," he says with a huge smile. "We're so glad to have you here."

"Thanks, Coach. I'm glad to be here."

Keller, of course, has apprised Coach Hartman of the issues I had at Idaho. He knows I was ineligible for three straight years. But he doesn't make me feel bad about any of it. Instead he just smiles and says to me, "Listen, we all make mistakes. That's part of life. But we're going to get you back on track. Believe me, you've got a lot of success ahead of you."

I am instantly invigorated. This is my kind of guy. A bright-side guy.

In five minutes, I already feel better than I've felt in years.

I've come to Spokane with absolutely nothing. No money. No place to stay. Luckily Hartman has set me up with the financial aid I couldn't get at Idaho and a part-time job in the school cafeteria, which will take care of my tuition and rent.

My new roommates are a shot-putter named Dennis Remley, a 400m runner named Micah Davis, and a decathlete named Kevin Moss. They seem like cool dudes, but like everyone, I'm sure they're sizing me up. On my first day of practice, I'm high jumping just as a warm-up, and slowly a crowd is starting to build. I know exactly what they're whispering.

"Hey, that's O'Brien. The guy from Idaho."

"Oh yeah. What's he doing here again?"

"I heard he flunked out."

"I heard he got busted for drinking."

"I wonder if he's any good."

To answer this final question, I clear six feet—then begin raising the bar. I clear 6-6, then 6-9, and now I've got everyone's attention. Nobody's talking anymore. All eyes are on me. I go 6-9, then 6-10, and now Coach Hartman has made his way over. When I go 6-11 everyone oohs and aahs, and when I just barely miss seven feet, I mean by a shoestring, even I can't believe how close I came to that mark. That's a huge jump at any level. I look over at Coach Hartman, who has a sly little smile on his face. Up until a few days ago he, was working with a stable full of quarter horses.

Now he's got himself a Seabiscuit.

Everything about junior college is easy for me. The classes, even for a slacker student like me, seem like a joke. I can't concentrate for shit and I don't study all that often, but I'm managing decent marks—mostly A's and B's on my early tests. And despite the fact that I haven't competed in an actual meet since high school, I'm pretty much dominating on the track. I'm doing a ton of single events. Long jump. Shot put. Discus. High jump. 100m. 400m. Hurdles. 4x4 relay. After coming off a three-year bender, you would think I'd be rusty. And in a lot of ways I am. But at a raw, fundamental level, this stuff just comes so naturally to me. I was born to be an athlete, and that makes up for a lot.

Halfway through the season we go to a meet at Boise State, where the University of Idaho team is competing, and against all these Division I guys, many of whom are my old teammates, I win three events and get named Athlete of the Meet. Keller's not surprised. He's always believed in my talent. At the conference championship, after I win the decathlon with a score of 7,275, I go on to win the 100m, long jump and the hurdles. And when it comes time for the 4 x 400 relay, even though I've done a ton of events and my shin splints are killing me, Coach Hartman wants me to run the anchor.

"If this thing comes down to the last leg," he says, "there's nobody I trust more."

To run a 400m right now, after all the events I've done, sounds like hell. But I don't want to let my coach down. When I get the baton, we're behind by about 15 meters, which I make up in the blink of an eye. With 100 meters to go I'm in the clear, pulling away from everyone, when suddenly my whole body locks up. My legs. My ass. The long day has finally caught up with me—as has the anchor from Clackamas College. I try to out-kick him to the line, because I want this race. I want it for my coach and my teammates. But as I'm about to find out, when you want things for other people, it's just not the same. You have to want it for yourself. With 10 meters to go, I pull up ever so slightly, and the kid from Clackamas drags me down for the win, making me realize, maybe for the first time, that I'm not invincible.

Still, we win the team title by a mile. And I had more than a little to do with it. After all my wins and that one second-place finish, I've scored 72 points all by myself, which is more than half of our team total, a feat virtually unheard of at any sort of college level. The next day the headline in the paper reads like this:

O'Brien Community College
Wins Conference Championship

So successful has my time in Spokane been that Washington State head coach John Chaplain, even though he knows I only have one year of eligibility remaining, has offered me a full scholarship for next season. I'm flattered, but I don't even consider it. The plan all along was for me to get my grades up to a point where I could return to Idaho, which I've done. After everything Keller's done for me, after all the times I've let him down, there's no way I can bail on him now. I've got a huge debt to pay.

9

It's the summer of 1988, and in an attempt to build on the momentum I created in Spokane, Keller thinks I should try to qualify for the Olympic trials in the decathlon. It's a long way from junior college competition, but the way I figure it, what the hell. The decathlon sucks, but what do I have to lose?

The last qualifying meet of the season is in Santa Barbara, California, where my Aunt Kay and Uncle Jim live in an absolute palace right on the beach. Auntie Kay is my dad's sister. Uncle Jim owned a cable TV company and sold it for millions. Their neighbor is the Shah of Iran, one of the richest men in the world, and their house is a full-blown compound on the majestic shores of the Pacific Ocean. The thing's got more bedrooms than a hotel, plenty of room for Keller and me and my dad, who has come down to watch the meet. I've barely seen him over the last two years.

"How ya been, Danny?" he asks.

"Good, Dad. Everything's going good."

For once, I'm actually not lying.

I have no intentions of winning this decathlon. There are legit pros here. My only goal is to somehow qualify for the Olympic trials, if only to appease Keller. As I'm warming up, my anxiety starts to bubble. A painful two days are in front of me. That's the thing about the decathlon: You know it's going to hurt. Like standing at the start line of a triathlon, you have to remind yourself why you're doing it.

After a so-so 100-meter, I long jump a huge personal best, almost 25 feet, and I close out with a 48.67 in the 400-meter, another personal best. Believe it or not, I'm in first place after Day One. As I'm walking through the parking lot with Keller and my dad, John Sayer, an older decathlete who nearly qualified for the '84 Olympic team, stops me. He calls me "Rook."

"Remember, Rook," he says, "this is a two-day event."

The general take on the decathlon is that the first day is the *athlete's* day, while the second day is the *decathlete's* day. In other words, while the first-day events cater more to raw speed and pure, explosive jumping prowess, the kind of traditional athleticism that a young, talented buck like myself has in spades, the second-day events are much more reliant upon the kind of skill and technique that can only come from years of practice and experience. The simple truth is you can be as good an athlete as you want, but you don't just pick up a pole and start vaulting 16 feet. You don't grab a javelin and throw 200 feet without some serious work. These are very awkward maneuvers that go against every athletic motion we learn growing up, the type of skills that are acquired over the course of a career, or even a lifetime—and as such, they provide three huge opportunities for an experienced guy like John Sayer to catch a "Rook" like me.

But that's not what happens.

John Sayer doesn't catch me.

Neither does anyone else.

I need to score 7,800 to qualify, and after running a giant PR in the 1500m with a time of 4:35.1, I'll be damned if I don't score 7,891 and win the thing outright. I beat all the pros, all the big-time college guys. In just my third decathlon since high school, after a four-year layoff, I've managed to qualify for the 1988 Olympic Trials.

Next stop, Indianapolis.

I have no clue how I'm going to pay for the trip to Indy. Plane tickets? Hotels? Who's going to cover all that?

"It's taken care of," Keller says.

"It is? How?"

"Don't worry about it."

"Are you paying?"

"I said don't worry about it."

"OK, whatever you say."

So we board a plane to the trials, which are being held at IUPUI (Indiana University-Purdue University Indianapolis), and from the minute I arrive there's a palpable feel that this is the big time. It's the first time I've ever had to wear a credential. ABC is televising. Flo Jo's here. Carl Lewis is here. When Keller spots Jackie Joyner-Kersee warming up, he says we have to meet her and Bob, her husband, who's also her coach. Bob is almost as big a presence as Jackie. They both command attention.

"I'd like you both to meet Dan O'Brien," Keller says, presenting me like merchandise.

"Hello, Dan," Jackie says. "It's good to meet you."

I'm nervous as all hell. I'm not even sure what I say.

"So, Dan," Bob interjects. "What event are you here for?"

"The decathlon."

He nods, asking me what I scored to qualify.

"7,891."

He nods again, like he's processing information, sizing me up. And then, as we all move to part ways to let Jackie get back to her warm-up, he says this: "I'm going to keep my eye out for you. I have a feeling you might do some things."

But not today.

I pull my hamstring in the long jump and have to drop out of the competition.

It's not terribly disappointing. In fact, it's a relief. I don't want to be a decathlete. I'm mostly here for Keller. I still think I can be a hurdler or a sprinter, either of which would keep me from having to go through this absolute grind that is the decathlon. If I can just get into the 26-foot range, maybe I can be a long jumper.

Or maybe not.

I told you about the long jump Carl Lewis pulled off in the rain here in Indianapolis. To see it live has had a life-changing impact on me. When he lands in the pit at almost 29 feet, I immediately said to myself, "I can't do that."

"I can get better. I can go 26, maybe even 27 feet. But I can't do that."

There's a big difference between selling yourself short and realizing your limits, and in this moment, I believe I have realized my limits. Not everyone can be Carl Lewis. I've always wanted to be that guy, but here, in the Indianapolis rain, I have come to grips with the fact that I'm not. My strength lies in my ability to be good at a lot of different things—my versatility—and when I really think about it, my enjoyment of diversity. How many football players stay out at halftime and do a trumpet solo? For as adamant as I've been in my disdain for the decathlon, maybe I've been suited for it all along.

Or maybe I'm just telling myself that.

Either way, I can't beat Carl Lewis. That much I know. And frankly, that's all I need to know. Right now the decathlon is wide open in America. There are some good athletes, for sure, but nobody is dominant. And nobody has my speed, which is the true X factor, the main component in as many as seven decathlon events. On speed alone I could likely hold my own as a professional right now. So my decision has been made. I'll do some single events in this last year of college, but from here on out, if I'm going to make a run at a real future in this sport, like it or not, it's going to be as a decathlete.

A few weeks after the trials, I'm back in Idaho and back to my old tricks. I'm over at Greg Bowen's place drinking beer, and when we're out, I volunteer to go to the store. It's right around the corner. Greg says I can take his truck.

"Careful of the brakes," he reminds me.

I slap a case of Keystone Light on the counter, hand the cashier a mess of wrinkled one-dollar bills and loose change, and jump back in the truck. I'm a hundred yards from the house when I take a corner too sharply. I try to pump the old dusty brakes, but nothing happens, and I'm going way too fast to make this turn. I crank the wheel as hard as I can, but I'm in too far. I'm headed straight for a parked car. There's no avoiding it. The crash booms against the silence of a Sunday afternoon in Moscow.

Fuck.

With school still a few weeks from starting, Moscow is like a ghost town. Not a single person on the sidewalk. Not a single car passing by. Not a single bird chirping. There's a light, almost eerie breeze in the air, making me feel like I've got about a hundred people quietly watching me from their living room windows. I look around again as I ponder my options: I could wait it out for the owner, which could be hours. I could leave a note with my name and number. Or I could flee the scene altogether. Greg's truck is pretty smashed up, at least the bumper, but the other car isn't all that bad, and I've got beer on my breath and a 12-pack sitting in the front seat.

Maybe it's best to run home, dump the beer, then come back and leave a note.

I run inside and tell Greg what has happened. He's not happy. I grab some paper and head out the front door, but as soon as I step outside, there's a police cruiser parked in the street and two officers walking up the driveway.

"This your truck?" one of the cops says, pointing to Greg's truck.

"No, it's a friend's."

"Well, we received a call that this truck was just in an accident. You know anything about that?"

Shit! Somebody *was* watching me!

"Actually, I can explain that," I say. "I was on my way back from the store, and the brakes on that old sucker aren't the best, and when I came around the corner I couldn't stop. I bumped into a parked car."

"So you left the scene of an accident?"

"No, not at all. I waited for like 30 minutes, and I was just on my way back to leave a note." I hold up the piece of paper and pencil as my proof.

"Have you been drinking?" the cop asks.

"What?"

"You heard me. Have you been drinking today?"

"Yeah, I've had a few beers. But I'm not drunk."

"So you were driving under the influence, *and* you left the scene of an accident?"

"I told you, I *didn't* leave the scene. Like I said, I was just on my way back to leave a note."

I hold the paper up again.

"Quit showing me that piece of paper," the cop says. "I don't care if you were going to leave a note or not. You left the scene of an accident. We're going to need you to take a Breathalyzer."

So now I'm in the back of a police cruiser headed down to the station, and for the life of me, I cannot believe what an idiot I am. After everything I've put myself and everyone around me through, after the third and fourth and fifth chances I've been given, I decide it's a good idea to drink and drive and leave the scene of an accident? The cops are right. It doesn't matter that I was planning to go back and leave a note, just as it doesn't matter that I've only had a few beers and think I'll pass a Breathalyzer. None of that is the point. The point is that I'm a fucking idiot. The point is that I continue to make these dumbass decisions like I can take them back whenever I want.

Snooping in the storage closet. Writing bad checks. Ditching class to smoke weed.

And now I can add a DUI to that list as I fail the shit out of the Breathalyzer.

I have no choice but to call Keller. I told him he could trust me. I promised him I would never let him down again. I know he's going to send me packing.

Clearing Hurdles

But instead, he does the opposite. He comes down to the station with a lawyer who starts barking about the way the cops brought me in, something about rights, and somehow gets my DUI reduced to a reckless driving right there on the spot. In addition, the hit-and-run has been completely erased. Never even happened. I end up with a suspended license, but I don't have a car, anyway. So fuck it. I'm off the hook. Keller has once again cleaned up my mess.

I owe this guy something major.

Once school starts up, Keller has me on the shortest leash you've ever seen. I might as well be wearing a shock collar. To keep tabs on my whereabouts, he arranges for me to live in the basement of an old lady's house across the street from him. He sets me up with a tutor to make sure I'm handling my schoolwork, and every day before practice, we meet in the library to go over notes from class. I can't blame him for taking everything out of my hands, as I've proven to be about as fit to handle myself as a two-year-old is to handle a loaded pistol.

Plus, it's working. By keeping me busy, by keeping me accounted for, I don't have any free time to screw things up. I go to school, I go to my tutor, I go to practice, and at night I'm back to officiating city league basketball games. Without a car, I run everywhere, all over town, my backpack filled with 20 pounds of books and a water bottle. I'm probably logging 10 or 20 miles a day when you factor in practice and the basketball games. When I get home at night I fall into my hide-a-bed like a tree, crashing off to sleep before my head hits the pillow. It feels good to actually be getting a few things done. At the end of the semester, I've kept my GPA where I left it in Spokane.

For the first time, I'm actually a member of the Idaho track team.

There are two seasons in college track, indoor and outdoor, and I roll through the indoor season without a hitch. At the Big Sky championships, I win the 55m hurdles and break the Kibbie Dome record by long jumping 25 feet, 10 inches, scoring the most points of anyone at the meet and qualifying for the NCAA national championships in Indianapolis. I'm excited for the trip, for the chance to win a national championship, but as it plays out, it's just not the University of Idaho's day.

It starts with our 800m runner, the only other Idaho athlete to qualify, Teddy Lindsley, who has a rare and untimely brain freeze when he thinks his race is over before it actually is. See, the track back in the Kibbie Dome— the track on which Teddy runs every single day—is an odd length, 300 meters, meaning an 800-meter run requires a bit more than two-and-a-half laps. But with the track here in Indy being a more conventional 200 meters, the race, instead, is a full four-lapper. Teddy knows this, of course, but as he's crossing the line on his third lap, in first place mind you, his instincts kick in for a split second and he pulls up, losing just a hair of his momentum. And that's all it takes. Virtually the entire pack slingshots past him, and just like that, in one false step, he's gone from first place to almost dead last.

After the race, understandably, he's sick at the thought of what just happened.

"It was right there for me," he says sadly, incredulously, putting his finger and thumb in the air, pinching them tight. "I was this close to a national championship."

Little do I know, I'm about to suffer an equally unfortunate fate.

First I don't even qualify for the long jump finals, despite going more than 25 feet, an almost unheard of scenario at the college level. And then, in the 55m hurdles, after I blow out of the blocks clean and assume the lead, the runner in the lane next to me crashes and takes me down with him, clipping the back of my heel. That's how quickly it happens in track. One step, one nanosecond, and everything you've worked for is gone.

Keller tries to protest the race, but it's not going to happen. It's over. I do make All-American, but it's little consolation.

"Don't worry," Keller says. "We'll get our national title in the outdoor season."

And for a while, it looks like I'm indeed going to make that happen. In early April I go to San Francisco State and score

Dan and Coach Keller

7,987 in the decathlon, the country's highest total for 1989. I'm the easy favorite to win the national championship, but as bad luck would have it, at the conference meet, just one week before the national championships, I rip the same hamstring I pulled at the '88 Trials and have no choice but to pull out.

I can't help but wonder if this is some kind of punishment, if karma is biting me in the ass for the last four years. I mean, hamstrings happen. But when the guy in the next lane crashes and takes you out with him? It's hard not to feel at least a little bit sour about that. Still, there's a bright side. I'm done with school, done struggling through something I'm not good at, and with a decathlon coming up that I've qualified to enter as a professional by way of having the highest collegiate score in the country, I've got an honest shot to do something. And after the shit I've put myself and everyone around me through, that's just about all I can ask for.

400-Meter

The most important thing in the Olympic Games is not to win but to take part, just as the most important thing in life is not the triumph but the struggle. The essential thing is not to have conquered but to have fought well.

This is the Olympic Creed, the pledge of the athlete, and never, in all my years, have I seen anyone embody it more than Derek Redmond. Derek is a 400-meter runner from Great Britain, and a damn good one. He broke the national record at 19, but at the 1988 Seoul Olympics he was forced to withdraw just 10 minutes before the final because of an Achilles injury. Here at the 1992 Barcelona Games, he has his shot at redemption. As one of the favorites for a medal, maybe even the gold, he runs the fastest time in the first round and wins his quarterfinal, and as I watch from the booth, I am struck by how good he looks. You hang around tracks long enough, and you can tell pretty easily who's ready to run fast.

But sports are fickle. And today, for whatever reason, just isn't Derek's day.

He comes out strong in the semifinal, but halfway into the race he comes skidding to a halt, clutching the back of his leg, his hamstring completely blown—and just like that, in one false step, his every Olympic dream is shattered. Again. He crumbles to the track in a heap of agony, and now the stretchers are being rushed out. Trainers circle around to help him up, but he waves them off. No stretchers. Not this time. He has already pulled out of one Olympics, and he's not about to do it again. He's going to finish this race if it kills him.

He pulls himself to his feet and begins hobbling along the rail, and the next thing you know, his father comes bolting out of the stands, blowing right past security and onto the track. He puts his arm around his son, and together, as 65 thousand people rise to their feet and begin cheering them on, they walk the last 150 meters. Derek is sobbing like a baby, and when his dad steps away to let him cross the finish line on his own, I honest-to-God have tears in my eyes. These people are cheering like they just watched a world record fall. Derek, of course, didn't break a world record. Nor did he win his race. Technically, he didn't even finish, as the rules say that a runner who is aided is officially disqualified. But nobody cares about that right now. Derek fought his guts out. He gave the people a reason to cheer.

Come to think of it, maybe today was his day, after all.

10

I get out of Ms. Keith's basement and move in with a guy named Sean O'Connor. We live in a shitty apartment in a shitty part of town known as "the ghetto." This is the life of an aspiring track-and-field athlete. There's nothing even remotely glamorous about it. You don't get drafted on ESPN. You don't sign some insanely huge contract. In fact, you don't sign any contract. You simply train your ass off, try to qualify for meets, and *if* you can afford the expenses, you show up and compete like hell for what little prize money is available. Perhaps if you win enough or somehow catch the eye of the right sponsor, you can land one of the few endorsement deals that are basically reserved for the top handful of athletes in the entire country. And until that happens, you work. Sometimes two jobs.

The road to track glory is not for the faint of heart.

In my case, in addition to working out all afternoon with Keller and the Idaho team, I wake up at 6 a.m. to load trucks for Culligan Water. Sometimes I go back at night. I also ref city-league basketball and put in 25 hours a week picking up range balls at the Idaho golf course. And still, I'm scraping to make rent. My roommate's pissed when we have to cancel our cable because I can't foot my half of the bill.

"I'm sorry, man. I'm broke."

And when I say broke, I don't mean things are a little tight. I mean I'm flat-on-my-ass broke. Without a car or even a license, I still run everywhere, and Keller, always the salesman, thinks there could be a way to use that to my advantage. If people knew my story, the kid they always see jogging down the street with a backpack on, they might be willing to help me out.

"I think you should go down to the Kiwanis luncheon," he says.

"The Kiwanis luncheon? For what?"

"To pitch yourself. Try to get one of these local businessmen to sponsor you. Tell them what you're trying to do. You never know, one of them just might give you some money."

"I don't know. I feel kind of weird about that."

"Look, this could really help you. As it is, you're spending more time running around town than you are at the track. How nice would it be to be able to train full time? Without distractions?"

He makes a good point, so I do it. I go to the luncheon, stand up in front of a bunch of suits, and deliver my pitch. "My name is Dan O'Brien. I'm a track-and-field athlete, and I'm trying to start a career. I think I can be pretty good, but I need money so I can train full time. I'm looking for some kind of sponsorship."

The room goes silent. Nobody's interested. Not even when I offer to make the investor a percentage owner in my future earnings.

It won't be long before they regret their decision.

It is the fall of 1989, and USA Track & Field has invited a group of decathletes to take part in a series of physical tests at the Olympic Training Center in Colorado Springs. I've done a few things to this point. I was All-American. I was a Junior Olympian. I had last year's top collegiate score. But that said, I haven't been invited for what I've done in the past. I've been invited for what people think I can do in the future, for my potential. I'm a legitimate 6-foot-10 high jumper, an easy 25-foot long jumper, a mid-to-low 10-second sprinter, and when an athlete of that caliber opts for the road less traveled, choosing the grind of the decathlon over one of the more glitzy single events, people notice.

Some of the tests they're putting us through are push-up and pull-up reps, speed and agility drills, Vo2 max, vertical leap and hand-eye coordination drills. To measure the latter, we go into a pitch-black room with about a thousand little lights shining on the walls. You're told to stare straight ahead, and when a light blinks, on either the right or left wall, you signal by raising the corresponding arm. My reaction time is the highest of anyone. In fact, all my numbers are through the roof. My vertical leap is an even 40 inches. My standing broad jump is almost 11 feet. Dave Johnson is the top-ranked American and the reigning U.S. champion, and it's not long before he approaches me.

"It's Dan, right?" he says.

"That's right."

He smiles, shakes my hand. "Well it's good to finally meet you, Dan. I'm Dave."

Hey, that has a nice ring to it.

"I know who you are, Dave," I smile back. "Congratulations on all your success."

"Well thank you. I appreciate that."

Dave is about as nice a guy as you're ever going to find. I mean really, genuinely nice, as humble as the day is long. He wears his love for the Lord on his sleeve, a sleeve he'd probably give you if you were even the slightest bit cold, but his kindness doesn't make him any less of a competitor. He wants to win.

He's on the lookout for threats, and he says he has a feeling about me. Says he can tell I'm coming for him. Says, "I think we're going to be seeing a lot of each other." He has no idea how right he is.

A few days after returning to Idaho, I pop in a tape of the 1987 World Championships in Rome, which I recorded when I was living in Spokane. Dave's competing, and I find that I can't take my eyes off him. In fact, I can't take my eyes off any of these guys, their struggle and fight glaringly evident in the driving Rome rain. This is the first time I've had an honest admiration for decathletes. To watch them splashing around the track in an inch of standing water, the pain and fatigue written all over their faces, is inspiring. East Germany's Torsten Voss runs undeterred, pure guts the main catalyst in a blistering 46-second 400m that helps propel him to a winning score of 8,680.

"Wow," I say to my roommate, Sean. "This Torsten dude is a complete stud."

Sean looks at Torsten, this hulking block of an Eastern European man who looks like he ought to be standing guard at the recently fallen Berlin Wall, and says, "Yeah, no way you could beat that guy."

I look at him sternly.

"What?" Sean says. "You think you could take that guy down?"

"I think I can break the world record."

Sean laughs. "Get out of here, O'Brien!"

"I'm serious. I think I can break Daley Thompson's record. 8,847."

Sean laughs again. "Man, you ain't never getting close to no 8,847."

Sean doesn't think anything of the exchange. To him, it's just banter, guys giving each other a hard time. He goes back to what he was doing like nothing has even happened, but for me, something *has* happened. Something has hit me: I need to be around people who believe in me. My first professional decathlon is only a few months away. I can't be dealing with anything that even resembles negative talk. Back when I was hanging with the locals, tripping out on mushrooms and smoking weed, Keller used to tell me that a man is, almost always, a product of who and what he surrounds himself with. So that's it. I can't be around here anymore. I can't live with Sean anymore. He's a good dude, but he's not on my page. A few days later I check on a small place closer to campus. It's not much, but it's all I can afford.

"I'll take it."

Then I go home, pack my two suitcases, and get the hell out of the ghetto.

Keller likes that I'm back living closer to campus now. This way he can monitor me better, taking me to and from practice, calling to make sure I didn't fall asleep after my morning shift at Culligan Water. He'd throw a fit if he knew I was still out partying and drinking a couple nights a week, if not more, so I do my best not to appear hung over the next morning.

When I was at the trials in Indy, I got a chance to see Flo Jo break the women's world record with a 10.49 in the 100m, which was faster than I'd ever run in my life. Relatively speaking, it was even more impressive than seeing Carl run that day at the Coliseum. She must've finished a good 25 or even 30 meters ahead of the field, and as I followed her down the track, I noticed something about the way she was running. She didn't look like the other runners. Her feet weren't pattering up and down like a rabbit in a fury. The word that came to mind was *bounding*. A cheetah bounding across an open prairie. She didn't pick her feet up and down as much as she sprang forward, her strides more of a long, powerful gallop. It looked effortless. Efficient. Even beautiful. I told myself that I want to run like that.

I work on it for the next six months, my workouts confined to the Kibbie Dome in the cold Idaho winter, the snow on the ground chewing into the golf course's hours, and thus, my paycheck. Even in a small apartment, I can't afford a big heating bill, so I sleep fully clothed with a wool hat beneath as many blankets as I can find.

It's hard to dream when you can see your breath.

But I'm looking toward April and my first postcollegiate meet, which is being held in Pullman on the campus of Washington State. When the day finally arrives, as usual, I'm a mess two hours prior, my nerves going haywire, which may or may not be the reason I get off to a shaky start with a 10.98 in the 100m, well off the 10.6 I've been averaging. But from there I absolutely take off, stringing together three consecutive personal bests—long jumping 26 feet, shot-putting an even 52 feet and high jumping 6-9. Those are huge numbers for any decathlete, let alone a young, inexperienced decathlete with just one year of collegiate competition under his belt.

I run 48.04 in the 400m to close out Day One in first place, and after beginning Day Two by hurdling a solid but not spectacular 14.41, I effectively end the competition with a 152-foot discus, extending my lead to a point where it doesn't even matter that I barely clear 14 feet in the pole vault or that my javelin dies out at 180 feet when some guys are going 210-plus.

I run 4:51.78 in the 1500-meter to finish almost dead last. I pace back and forth with my hands on my head gasping for air, grimacing in pain, but when it's all said and done, I have won my first attempt at a professional decathlon with a score of 8,267. So far this year it's the top score in America, trumping my personal best by more than 400 points, and Keller and I couldn't be more excited—though the root of our excitement is, I think, somewhat different. Keller, of course, is excited that I won. He sees big things for me, always has, and maybe this is a start to making all the shit I've put him through a little more worth it. Maybe, just maybe, there's a chance I'm going to pay him off after all.

My excitement, on the other hand, isn't so much a product of my winning as it is the simple fact that this thing is finally over. I'm happy that I won, sure. But this is a brutal price to pay for a few moments of satisfaction. My muscles feel like jelly, like they're about to slide right off my bones, my shaking quads making it a challenge to even walk. If I said before that the decathlon feels like a cross-country flight with 10 layovers, I have to say, I badly misspoke. That may have been true in high school and even college, but at this level, when you're not just going through the motions of the events, when you're drawing upon every ounce of focus and explosion you have because now you're chasing a score, a career, a life, it feels more like an around-the-world flight with 10 layovers in six different time zones, the jet lag making you downright dizzy.

My body is mush. So is my mind. And for that, I get exactly zero prize money. Not one dollar. In fact, my only reward, if you can even call it that, is that I get to do it again, as my score has qualified me for the U.S. Championships in June. It's a big deal. For the sheer collection of talent on display, many people consider the U.S. Championships to be the most impressive track meet in the world, even more so than the Olympics, if only for the fact that the athlete who can't crack the top three or four in America is often good enough to make just about any other Olympic team on the planet.

Which is precisely why John Chaplain thinks I'm in for a rude awakening.

John Chaplain, if you'll remember, is the Washington State coach who offered me the scholarship after my year in Spokane—and he's nothing if not the most straightforward, no-bullshit guy you've ever met in your life. While everyone else is congratulating me on my effort, pretty much telling me how great I did, John, instead, flags me down and says this:

"So listen, O'Brien—your pole vault and javelin are for shit."

Jesus. Tell me what you really think.

"If you want to do this thing, I mean for real," he goes on, "then you have to get better in those last few events. Either that, or guys are going to drag you down from behind. Mark my words. These guys here couldn't catch you, but when you get up there with the big boys, it's going to be a whole different story. You need to talk with Sloan. He's the guy to help you."

Rick Sloan, a former decathlete who finished seventh at the '68 Olympics, is the field-events coach at Washington State, and he's quickly earning a reputation for being the guy behind a lot of really top-notch hammer and discus throwers and high-jumpers. I've met him in passing at a few track meets and on that trip to Indy last year, but I don't know a whole lot about him. Neither does Keller, who normally isn't the type of guy to give up control. But we intend to make a serious run at this thing. We're not screwing around. And if Sloan can help, what do we have to lose?

Keller works out all the arrangements and then informs me of the plan: For the next few months, between now and the U.S. Championships, I'll spend the mornings, after work, doing my running work with Keller in the Kibbie Dome. Then, in the afternoon, I'll drive the eight miles across the border to Pullman to work with Sloan and his Washington State guys. Keller says I can use his spare truck, a little beat-up Toyota, which is such a shitbox that you don't even need a key to start it. Just your thumb in the ignition will do.

"Oh, by the way," Keller adds, "you made Frank Zarnowski's newsletter."

He says it nonchalantly, but again, it's a big deal.

Considered the world's foremost decathlon authority, Frank Zarnowski, an economics professor by day, is Coach Hunt times a thousand—the nut of all decathlon nuts. Back in the late '60s, when decathletes composed what was still a largely underground athletic society (not that they still don't), Frank wound up meeting a young collegiate decathlete by the name of Bill Walsh. Oddly enamored with Bill's unique, if unappreciated skill, Frank personally organized a meet, getting a sanction and everything, to provide this Walsh kid with an opportunity to achieve the qualifying standard for the 1968 Olympic team. Bill didn't make the standard, but nevertheless, Frank was hooked. The decathlon had become the source of his greatest fascination. In a 1979 *Sports Illustrated* feature, he called it the event of Renaissance men.

For years he was virtually alone in his admiration for decathletes, who had historically existed in almost total obscurity, like Kenyan distance runners, second-class citizens to the more celebrated sprinters and long jumpers. The first time the decathlon garnered any sort of television coverage was at the 1960 Olympics in Rome, where Rafer Johnson won gold by outdueling his UCLA teammate C.K. Yang, and it wasn't until the spring of 1970 that the NCAA finally included it as part of its national championships.

Frank, as it turns out, happened to be at that meet, which was being held in St. Paul, Minnesota. He was only there as a fan, but when the decathlon started he decided to walk down to the track, where he noticed an unmanned, live microphone. He picked it up, and without invitation, began announcing. To his surprise, nobody objected, probably because nobody else knew shit about the decathlon, and shortly thereafter USA Track & Field began paying his way to meets as the official decathlon announcer. Soon he was writing decathlon books and teaching a two-unit college course on decathlon appreciation. But what he's probably most known for is his monthly decathlon newsletter, *DECA*, which has become the thread that connects all the world's decathlon nuts. And there are more of them than you might think.

As *Sports Illustrated* noted, you're liable to read anything in these newsletters—that just 55 men have topped the 8,000-point mark since the first Olympic decathlon in 1912; that 5,471 is the highest score ever tallied by a native of the Fiji Islands; that Harry Marra, now the head coach at San Francisco State, ranks fifth, at right about 140 pounds, on the all-time points-per-pound record list. You want to know who's scoring what and where they're doing it? Check the newsletter. You want to know about upcoming events? Check the newsletter. I'm telling you, these things are like decathlon scripture. Everyone gets them. Everyone reads them. So to see my name next to the top American score for the year of 1990 feels like the coolest thing ever. This is my announcement, my coming-out party, my official arrival on the decathlon scene.

I show up for my first day with Sloan thinking I'm really something.

For starters, I saunter in about 15 minutes late, which is the worst first impression I could've possibly made. As I'll learn very quickly, Sloan, who's only in his mid 40s but feels much more old school than that, doesn't have a single shred of patience for showing up late. I haven't even stepped in the batter's box yet, and already I have a strike.

"You ready to go?" Sloan asks me in a serious, don't waste-my-fucking-time tone.

"Yeah. I'm ready."

"Good, then let's do it."

I head off with some javelin throwers, and for a while, Sloan just observes. He makes a few comments here and there, but mostly he just wants to see me throw, just to see what he's working with. Years later he will tell me that he knew I could be the best athlete in the world this very first day he saw me work out. He will tell me that in all his years around the sport, never had he seen someone with so much natural ability, and that deep down, he was already thinking about the heights to which we could soar together.

But I'd never know it in a million years.

Unlike Keller, who pretty much babies me, arranging for me to get to and from places, checking in on my whereabouts, giving me second and third and fourth chances because he knows what I'm capable of, Sloan's not going to stand for any of my shit. He doesn't work that way. When he sees me checking my watch about an hour into our workout, he calls me right on it.

"You got someplace to be?"

"Huh?"

"I see you checking your watch. You have an appointment or something?"

"Actually, I have a tee time," I say.

"As in, a *golf* tee time?"

"Yeah. I'm playing with a couple buddies at the course I work at."

"Well," he snickers, "I guess you better get going then. I know how you hate to be late for things."

Touché.

"No, it's OK," I say. "I can stay."

"All right, listen," Sloan says, fed up. "You need to ask yourself a question right now. Do you want this or not?"

"Of course I do."

"Because if you don't," he continues, "if you'd rather be off playing golf, then I have better things to do, too."

"OK. I understand. Forget the tee time."

"It's not just the tee time. I can't want this more than you do. Nobody can. You have to want this for yourself."

"I do. Believe me."

"And while we're at it," he says, as though he's barely hearing my answers, "I have a few ground rules if we're going to work together. First, show up on time. If something's important enough, you'll find a way to be on time. And second, don't show up to a workout hung over or not ready to get after it. When you walk onto the track or into the weight room, I expect that you're ready to work."

Again, I tell him I understand, and again, he barely hears me. Truth be told, he doesn't care what answers I give him. I can see all over his face exactly what he's thinking.

Actions speak louder than words.

Men at Work: Dan and Sloan

11

It's June 12, 1990, and I'm at the U.S. Championships at Cerritos College in Norwalk, California. It's my first meet with Sloan in my corner. We've been working together for about a month now, and I think I'm proving something to him. I think he can see that not only am I willing to work, but I also seem to have a greater capacity for it than most. He's made comments about my remarkable recovery rate, about how I can work myself to the bone and come back the very next day ready to go again.

A few days before the decathlon, Keller says a Nike rep wants to meet with me.

"Seriously? Are they going to give me some money?"

"I don't know," Keller says. "Let's just take the meeting."

We go to the guy's hotel room, but before I can even get my hopes up, he tells me that with Dave Johnson already on board, they're not looking to bring on another decathlete at the moment. "But," he says, "you're definitely on our radar. We'd like to at least get you set up with some gear."

I'd rather you set me up with some money.

"Here," he says, tossing me a singlet. "Try this on."

And while you're at it, try this. And this. And this. I end up walking out of that room with so much Nike shit that I look like I looted a Foot Locker. Javelin boots. Sprint shoes. Long jump spikes. Running tights. Windbreakers. I at least look the part by the time Day One rolls around, and if nothing else, I now have a lot more incentive to perform well. If I can go big in this thing, put up a number and finish in the top two or three, maybe I'll get some sponsorship. Maybe I can stop dragging my ass around the driving range in that cart that golfers like to aim at.

Keller and Sloan give me some time alone before my first event, and it's all I can do to not vomit. That it's the U.S. Championships, the biggest event of the year, only adds to the premeet anxiety that has become as much a part of my routine as stretching. I can't stop thinking about that fucking 1500-meter.

I know I shouldn't be looking that far ahead. I know the Tour de France riders aren't thinking about that last vertical climb up the winding face of a mountain before Stage One even starts. Or are they? How can they not? I sure as hell would be. Hell, even when I play Mario Bros. I find myself worrying about the beast at the end before I've even made it through the first level.

That's what the 1500 is to me: the beast at the end of the game. It breathes fire.

"You ready?" Keller asks me.

Ready as I'll ever be.

When we walk out to the track, everyone's cracking jokes about how few people are in the stands.

"Looks like somebody's family showed up," Dave Johnson laughs.

As a decathlete, you get used to this right away. You don't have thousands of fans to get you pumped up. You have to find your fuel inside. I bet there aren't more than a few hundred people here, but I'm ready to go. Once I get past the jitters, I'm

Dan and Dave Johnson, 1990

always excited at the start of a decathlon, because right away I've got two of my best events. It gives me a chance to get out early, create some momentum for myself, and maybe put a few guys on their heels in the process.

But I've never come out like this.

First I run 10.4 in the 100-meter, blowing everyone clean out of the water, and then I follow that up by damn near breaking the decathlon long jump world record with a mark of 26 feet, 5 inches. These are the best decathletes the United States has to offer, and suddenly they're all chasing *me*, the guy who's competed in exactly one professional decathlon. I notch another personal best with a big 6-foot-10 high jump that very easily could've been bigger, my heel barely scraping the bar on my way over seven feet, and after running a 49-second 400m, I end Day One with a giant lead.

Clearing Hurdles

"Don't even look at the scoreboard," Keller reminds me. "Just keep the pedal down."

It's easier said than done. I'm one day from winning a U.S. Championship. But Dave Johnson is a notoriously big second-day guy, a monster pole-vaulter and javelin thrower, a proven finisher in the cruel and unusually punishing 1500. As the defending champion, he knows how to win, and there's a lot more than you think to be said for that. To have won at this level before is to know you can do it again, no questions, no doubt, and pretty simply, I'm not at that place yet.

I start Day Two decently well, hurdling 14.01 and throwing a 150-foot discus to pretty much maintain my lead. And then I hang on for dear life. I pole-vault 4 meters 30, just over 14 feet, while Dave booms almost a 17-footer—and the gap closes. I go 190 in the javelin, not bad, but Dave launches one well over 220 feet.

"Johnson delivers a big throw!" Frank Zarnowski says over the loudspeaker.

And just like that, my lead has vanished. Dave has done what champions do: He's been patient in his kill, applying constant, steady pressure, like a python slowly squeezing the life from my lungs. And now he's got me. Now the only way out of his grip is to not only beat him in the 1500, but beat him by an appreciable nine seconds, which seems like an impossible feat. Dave's a seasoned, proven 1500-meter runner, while I'm scared to death of this thing. I've never gone lower than 4:35 in my whole life, yet Keller thinks we need to go at least 4:25 to have a realistic shot. So basically, I'm fucked.

Keller and Sloan are clamoring on about race strategy, their feet tapping nervously as they try to throw together a last-second plan. What do I need to run? When do I need to make my push? And what about a pacesetter? Is there anyone I can follow? Anyone I can ride to the time I need? For all of Sloan's experience, both as an athlete and a coach, none of us has ever been in a situation like this. Down to the last event with a shot at winning the U.S. Championship? This is completely uncharted territory. And our inexperience is really showing.

Everyone's hemming and hawing. Nobody's making any decisions, least of all me. I'm sitting in the corner completely intimidated and utterly exhausted. Today I spent four hours in the pole vault alone. Took 14 jumps. At this point, I just want this godforsaken race to be over. I can already hear the ring of the last-lap bell—the one that sends honest shivers up my spine, the one letting me know I've still got 400 meters to go when I can hardly breathe—and it's making me sweat cold.

As I stand up from my final stretches, I say, "Let's get this over with."

And so the gun goes off, and I'm not ready. I'm not ready to race, and I'm sure as hell not ready to win something as big as a U.S. Championship. Not yet. I run 4:43 to Dave's 4:35 to finish in second place with a score of 8,403, besting my Pullman performance by almost 200 points. All things considered, as I go to one knee completely out of breath, I'm pretty happy. I think Sloan and Keller are, too. After all, finishing second at the U.S. Championships in just your second professional decathlon isn't anything to mope about.

I look for the Nike guy, thinking maybe I might've impressed him enough to warrant some kind of deal. But he's nowhere to be found. In baseball or basketball a guy might be able to make some real money as a role player, playing 10 or 15 minutes a game or pinch-hitting twice a week, but in track and field, for

Clearing Hurdles

the most part, there's the best and then there's everyone else. The best get paid, and everyone else goes back to the driving range.

The University of Washington is the site of the 1990 Goodwill Games, and it has all the feel of a big international event. Athletes are here from all over the world. Before my competition starts, I head over to watch Jackie Joyner-Kersee in the 100m hurdles, the first event of the heptathlon, which is the female version of the decathlon— seven events instead of 10. Jackie is the greatest female athlete of all time, even better than Flo-Jo. At the 1986 Goodwill Games, she became the first woman to score over 7,000 points in the heptathlon, and two years later, at the 1988 Olympics in Seoul, she went 7,291 to set a record that might never be broken. At those same games she set an Olympic long jump record with a mark of 24-3, and for good measure, she even starred as a basketball player at UCLA. I find a seat just as the track announcer introduces her to a buzzing crowd.

"Ladies and gentlemen," he says, "in Lane 4, out of Los Angeles, California . . ."

And from there he breaks into the résumé: *two-time Olympic gold medalist. Two-time world champion. Eight-time U.S. champion. World record. Olympic record. American record.* The list never stops, and it occurs to me that this has to be the truest measure of greatness: an introduction that takes so goddamn long to get through that the announcer has to pause to take a breath before finishing.

In seeing and hearing the way the crowd reacts to Jackie, in feeling the anticipation in the air as her race nears, I realize that it isn't so much the event that the fans come out to watch.

It's the athlete. The star power. In theory, the heptathlon should be as long and boring to watch as the decathlon, but because of Jackie, the people come out. She's the star power that the decathlon is lacking. She has made the multi-events competition cool, and that's what I want to do. I want to be the male Jackie Joyner-Kersee.

My family has made the trip up to Seattle, but I don't concern myself with them. The night before Day One I need some space. This is something Keller and Sloan have yet to fully figure out about me, that my heart races long before my legs, and that rather than try to rein me in and keep me close, it's best to just let me go. Let the nerves run their course. I think I could be around them if they could somehow keep from talking about the very thing that's making me anxious, but they can't. When we were in Norwalk for the U.S.

Coaches Keller and Sloan

Clearing Hurdles

championships, I swear, on the night before Day One, they couldn't go more than 10 minutes without mentioning something decathlon related. *Remember to stay balanced in the shot put. Don't go out too early in the 400.* I could hear the anxiety in their voices, see it on their faces, which made me even more nervous than I already was.

Fortunately, I don't have to worry about any of that here in Seattle. I'm staying in the athletes' village, the university dorms, while Keller and Sloan are in a hotel. As I lay in bed on the eve of Day One, I can see them biting their fingernails to the bone.

To make a long story short, I don't have nearly as strong a first day in Seattle as I did in Norwalk. I run 10.99 in the 100m, and though I start the 400 in a blaze, I go out too fast, too hard, and die down the stretch for a 48.38. My shot put and high jump are so-so, and I hurdle a very average 14.44. And yet, I actually have an even bigger lead than I did at the U.S. Championships. I haven't had any great events, but I haven't had any terrible ones, either and sometimes that's what it takes.

But once again, here comes Dave.

While I barely manage to vault 14 feet before throwing a 190-foot javelin, Dave goes 4 meters 95 in the pole vault (16 ¼ feet) and throws a big 225-foot javelin to all but erase my lead. Heading into the 1500m, my margin is six seconds. That's what it comes down to. If I can stay within six seconds of Dave, I'll win.

"With everything on the line, Dave's going to go hard," Keller says. "I think we need to go at least 4:28. I think that's our number."

Oh, just 4:28? Is that all?

"Yeah," Sloan concurs. "That should be enough."

So 4:28 it is. It's doable, if you don't mind the feeling of an ice pick stabbing you in the throat. It at least makes me feel better that we're not going into this thing blind. Since the U.S. meet, we've started looking around at what other guys are running, personal bests and average times, and here in Seattle we've even hooked up with a pacesetter—Michael Smith from Canada, who's still in the running for a bronze but has no chance of catching me, and therefore has no problem helping me. Michael says he's going to run 68-second laps. It's a 4:15 pace if sustained, and since Mike is one of those guys who usually comes pretty close to his number, I, in turn, should get pretty close to mine if I can stay within 25 meters of him.

"You feel good about that?" Keller asks me.

It's a tough question. Yes, I do feel good that we have an actual plan. But no, I don't feel good about this race. I never feel good about this race. As I start my warm-up, the anxiety kicks in like a reflex. I know I have to run what basically equates to a 4:30 mile. I know it's going to hurt like hell. And I no doubt make it even worse in my head, like I'm being asked to run barefoot over a bed of burning coals. So irrational am I when it comes to the 1500m that in the moments preceding the race, I actually start to contemplate other careers. I tell myself I can't go through this feeling of agony and dread for even one more minute. I start to wonder what kind of job I could get without a college degree, and just as I'm running through a pretty bleak list of options, just as I round out of my final warm-up lap, I see Dave and his guys holding hands in the corner with their heads bowed and eyes closed in one final prayer.

Terrific.

Clearing Hurdles

Coach Rick Sloan

As if beating Dave wasn't going to be hard enough, now I have to beat God, too.

With the Almighty on his side, Dave again is way too much for me in the 1500. I run for all I'm worth, going out in a respectable 4:36, which is a full eight seconds better than my time in Norwalk and just one second off my personal best, but Dave blows the doors off with a 4:26 to finish with a score of 8,403. I go 8,358 to finish alone in second. Smith does exactly what he said he was going to do, going out in 4:23, but it's not enough to hold off Russia's Mikhail Medved, who finishes in third with a score of 8,330, thanks to a giant discus and pole vault.

"Give it time," Sloan reminds me. "We're just getting started."

By way of my two second-place finishes and my victory in Pullman, I am going to end this year ranked No. 2 in America (behind Dave) and No. 4 in the world. Is that some shit or what? My first season as a pro, after just one year of college competition, and I'm the No. 4-ranked decathlete in the world. When I really stop and think about it, I can't help but feel good. I have exceeded even my own lofty expectations, and more importantly, the expectations of my mom. Quietly, I think I've always wanted to prove to her that I could be the one in her 1-

in-10,000 statistic, and what says you've made it more than walking around on the same track as Carl Lewis? That's what really made it register for her. Even my mom knows Carl. When they hang the silver medal around my neck and present me with a handful of flowers, I look at her. She's smiling. She's proud. When I get back in the stands, I give her the flowers and kiss her on the cheek.

"I can't believe it," she says, shaking her head.

"What can't you believe?"

"That you're really doing this. All these years, I always thought you were just playing games. But this is, like, for real."

"Yeah, Mom. It is real. I told you I was going to do something someday."

"Yes," she says with a smile, almost crying. "You sure did."

Dan and Dave with the greats

12

Sloan likens a day of decathlon training to an honest day of hard, blue-collar work. In the trenches. Down and dirty. Grab your lunch pail and hardhat and prepare to be flat-on-your-ass exhausted come day's end.

Back in Pullman, it's time to go to work. And it starts with the javelin.

At the moment, I'm averaging about 190 feet, which, given the lack of coaching I've had in this event, is actually pretty decent. But it's not even close to what Dave and some of the other big guns are throwing. Sloan says I'm getting by on my natural, fast-twitch explosion at the point of release, but my technique all the way up to that point is for shit. The javelin, as I said earlier, is an acquired, awkward mechanism, and though I've picked up a lot on my own, there are still remaining pieces of the natural motion you learn as a kid throwing baseballs and newspapers. Sloan and I are starting from the ground up.

Short run-up–three to five steps–plant your foot in the ground and turn your hips.

"That's what you want to be thinking about," Sloan says, pressing his left foot firmly against the ground, slapping his hand hard against his quad to reinforce stability. "Stick that foot in the ground, and turn your hips hard."

The idea is to not allow your momentum to carry you through your throw, to not jump off the ground like I tend to do—but rather, to stop on a dime, plant that foot to create an axis, then turn over it. It's like a pitcher coming down out of his motion, all that energy coming to a halt as he sticks his foot in the dirt and lets his hips and shoulders fire open. It's a powerful, violent action, and I'm repeating it over and over, throw after throw, day after day. And it's not long before I start to see the fruits of my labor, my jav cutting through the air cleaner, crisper, getting out beyond 190 feet despite the short run-up.

"Turn!" Sloan instructs as I launch another, and another, and another. "Turn hard!"

One day I fire my best throw yet, screaming through my release, holding my finish against a firmly planted front side.

"Bam!" Sloan yells, clapping his hands together hard. "There it is. You feel that?"

I do feel it. Something has clicked. That's how it happens with the javelin, and I guess with a lot of other events; you work and try things out and figure it out little by little, and then boom, one day it just happens. Everything adds up. Makes sense. Sloan has a way of explaining things, and I have a way of understanding and applying them. It will prove to be a deadly combination.

Of course, the decathlon is a life lesson in the art of balance. You can't spend all your time in one place. You're a juggler, a single mom with a full-time job, 10 different things to do with not nearly enough time in the day—and right now, my pole vault shortcomings are second only to my 1500m, which I don't even really account for in my training. I just hang on for all I'm worth in that fucker.

"Tell me what you're thinking about when you vault," Sloan says.

"I don't know," I say. "It happens so fast. I guess I'm not thinking anything."

Sloan laughs. "That's actually good in a lot of ways," he says. "But I'm going to give you just a few things to think about. First, keep your hands high. Away from your body. When we're a little unsure, a little bit scared, our protective instinct is to pull our hands in close and tight, but that's how the pole ends up controlling you. You want the opposite. You need to control the pole. You need that room to operate. So keep those hands high. And penetrate. That's the other thing. The more penetration, the better."

Vaulters hear this word a lot. Penetrate. Much like your plant leg in the javelin, when you're vaulting, you want to plant the pole hard and jump into it, through it, like a boxer punching all the way through his opponent's chest rather than stopping on contact. That's penetration. That's what causes the pole to bend and thrust you not just upward, but forward, rather than sending you straight up and straight back down.

"Make sense?" Sloan says.

"I don't know," I joke. "I'll tell you in a minute."

Sloan smiles. I laugh. Our chemistry is developing by the minute. I charge down the runway with something to prove to him, something to prove to myself. He stands right at my take-off point, putting his hand under me for a little extra push just as I leave the ground.

"Hands high!" he yells as I go again, and again, and again. "Penetrate!"

Sloan was a monster pole-vaulter in his day. In practice he would regularly set the bar upwards of 17½ feet, which at that time was a world-record height. In fact, his training partner, a pole-vaulting legend by the name of Dick Railsback, actually owned the world record for a short period. So Sloan was right there with the best. I think he cleared 17-2 as his PR, which seems skyscraper high to me. I'm setting the bar at 15-3, 15-4, maybe 15½, and the higher I go, the scarier it gets.

"You have to trust it," Sloan says. "The pole vault is all about trust."

That's easy to say, but for me, and for almost every young vaulter, there's nothing easy about sticking the pole in the ground at full speed and launching yourself 15 or 16 feet into the air, let alone upside down. The tendency is to want to slow down, to ease up just that little bit at the very last second, to go into your vault cautiously, hesitantly, like a motorcycle rider letting off the throttle just before he hits the big ramp. But this is the absolute wrong thing to do. If anything, you want to pick up speed. But the only way to do that, again, is to trust that everything's going to be OK, that you're going to make it over the bar and into the pit without killing yourself.

And the only way to gain that trust is to do it over and over and over again.

"Repetition," Sloan says. "Repetition, repetition, repetition."

We jump almost every day. We're determined to break through this wall. And I can feel it working. Before long I'm pushing my vaults up near 16 feet, and I've taken my work in the gym to another level. This, I think, is the foundation for the immediate connection Sloan and I have found: our love for the workout. It's strange, I realize, that I have such a passion for training yet dread the actual decathlon, for the training, clearly, is a thousand times more painful. But the training is also pressure free. To be in the gym or on the track with sweat dripping from my brow, with my shirt soaked through, with my heart pounding, gives me a feeling of absolute strength, absolute purity, and I've become impossibly addicted to that feeling. And Sloan's the same way.

Everyone knows about his "noon-time" workouts. Every day at noon on the dot, come hell or high water, Sloan is running. Lifting. If you don't show up, he still runs. Still lifts. He remains an athlete at heart, a grinder, a man who would never ask one of his athletes to do something he wasn't willing to do himself. And you can't help but want to show up for a guy like that.

Hell, I wish I could spend even more time training, but unfortunately, I still have to work. Is that some shit or what? I'm the fourth-ranked decathlete in the world, and I'm still unloading water trucks and picking up golf balls. In fact, since I still owe the university almost five grand, I've taken on even more work, painting and pulling weeds at apartment complexes for six bucks an hour. I won $1,500 for placing second at the Goodwill Games, and USA Track & Field spotted me a $1,200 grant for my showing at the U.S. Championships. But I'm still barely making rent.

Like I said before, this lack of financial support isn't a problem specific to me. It's a problem for just about all decathletes, or really, all track-and-field athletes, period. Bart Goodell was once a promising decathlete who lived out of his car for the better part of a year while training for the '88 Olympics. You hear stories like this all the time. America has the proudest decathlon tradition in the world, more gold medalists than any country in the world. But we're slipping. We haven't won a gold medal since Jenner in 1976. And how can we expect that to change if our youngest and brightest decathletes are living in a car? If they're only able to train between shifts at the supermarket?

Enter the Visa Decathlon Program.

I've been hearing rumblings about it for the last year and a half, ever since that trip to the Olympic Training Center, but now it's official. Visa has agreed to sponsor a national decathlon team by providing a level of financial and professional support the likes of which no American decathlete has ever known. I'm talking monthly stipends to everyone ranked in the top 10. Access to national coaches and sports psychologists. Training clinics. Travel expenses. The very best in sports medicine. Historically, the decathlete's Olympic quest has been largely, if not entirely, solitary—the longest and loneliest of journeys. And for the most part, it'll remain that way. Guys will still hide away with their coaches and closest confidants and go about their training with only the sun as a clock. But now, with this Visa Decathlon Program, there will at least be a support system in place. Resources. A little change in your pocket. Likeminded people who are going to be in your corner, who are going to be there to listen if you need them, who are going to do everything they can to help you get where you're trying to go.

Even when you're alone, it feels good to know that you're not alone.

I, of all people, know that.

The kickoff event is being held in the spring of 1991 at the San Francisco Marriot. It's by far the nicest place I've ever stayed. Looks like a big jukebox. Just as I'm about to go inside, I hear some commotion behind me, and when I turn around, I see the one and only Bruce Jenner pulling up in a cable car with his gorgeous wife, Kris Jenner. Together, with their lightbulb smiles and perfect hair, they look like movie stars—and really, they might as well be. Kris is a the embodiment of a Hollywood queen, and Bruce, with his heartland roots that trace back to Iowa's tiny Graceland College, is the classic All-American story. He's the small-town kid who ran his way to the 1976 Olympic gold medal, to the front of the Wheaties box, and to watch him navigate a room is to watch an absolute professional celebrity. He's shaking hands. Smiling for pictures. Reveling in the glow of the spotlight. I'm in complete awe, studying him from afar, when I feel a tap on my shoulder.

It's Fred Samara.

"Dan O'Brien," he says with a big smile. "How the hell are you?"

"I'm good, Fred. Real good."

Fred is the track coach at Princeton, and along with San Francisco State's Harry Mara, he'll be serving as the Visa program's national coach. He was a hell of a decathlete in his day, an NCAA and U.S. champion, while Harry, as you might remember, ranks fifth on Frank Zarnowki's all-time points-per-pound record list. The three of these guys have kind of a cool connection, as back in the early 70s, when Fred and Harry were still competing and Frank was announcing, they used to room together on the road. At night they would sit up trying to think of ways to promote this event they all loved so much. To think a big company like Visa would one day throw millions of dollars into the decathlon would've been beyond their wildest dreams.

"I wanted to congratulate you on all your success," Fred says. "We've got high hopes for you."

As the second-ranked American, a lot of people are looking at me now. Somebody has to validate this program and return the gold medal to America, and if not Dave, then who more likely than the guy who finished right on his tail at the last two major meets?

"Thank you," I say. "I appreciate that. This is pretty exciting."

"I know, right? I'm really looking forward to hearing some of the guys speak."

Fred is referring to what's being hyped as the Gold Medal Panel, which consists of the five living American decathletes to have won the gold medal. Bob Mathias, who won the first of his back-to-back golds when he was just 17. Milt Campbell, the first black man to win the Olympic decathlon. Rafer Johnson, probably the best pure athlete of the group and star pupil of the legendary Ducky Drake. Bill Toomey, "Wide World of Sports" Athlete of the Year for 1968. And of course, Jenner. Still the iconic face of the American decathlon.

We all gather in a big ballroom. Zarnowksi is the emcee, and after introducing some of the Visa folks, including John Bennett, the man who really gave this program legs, he says, "And now, let's all stand and give a warm welcome to our Gold Medal Panel!"

My eyes dart to the entrance. I've been waiting anxiously for this moment ever since I got the invite to this thing. I was never one to voluntarily pick up a book in school, but since fully committing myself to the decathlon, I've started to read up on all the guys who came before me. I'm beginning to see why Coach Hunt and Frank Zarnowski are so fascinated by decathletes. In their pictures they look like gladiators from another time, stone-faced and square-jawed, statuesque men with broad, chiseled physiques.

This is how I have them built up in my head. But anymore, this is not who they are.

At least not to look at them.

Jenner, tall and handsome, still looks the part, but the other guys look, well, ordinary, like someone you might pass in a coffee shop—Toomey the embodiment of a six-foot everyman. You can tell Rafer was an athlete in his day, but he's so much skinnier than I would've thought. It's hard to believe this is the same guy who was offered a role in *Spartacus*, the guy who played basketball for John Wooden at UCLA. And Milt Campbell? The guy once cut from the mold of a Greek god? The guy who nearly qualified for the Olympics in both judo and swimming and later played football for the Cleveland Browns? He must be pushing 300 pounds. He looks like he's about to deliver twins.

All I can think is, *These are the world's greatest athletes?*

Even though I know these guys are getting up there in age, I'm still surprised. Still disappointed. But then they start talking, start telling their stories, and soon I begin to see that my preoccupation with these guys' muscles has caused me to miss their true strength. Hell, listen to the tale of Bill Toomey: In 1967 he came down with some sort of mystery illness while competing in Europe. Doctors had no idea what was wrong with him, but he couldn't get out of bed for a month. Finally, on sheer will, he forced himself to the track, where he was barely able to walk a single lap. Less than a year later, he broke the world decathlon record by running 45.68 in the 400m en route to winning the 1968 gold medal in Mexico City.

There's no excuse good enough for these guys. No challenge from which they would ever shrink. Milt Campbell dedicated himself to becoming an All-American swimmer after he was told black people had no place in the water. In fact, he wound up breaking the New Jersey state records of the kid who said it.

"Don't ever let anyone tell you that you can't do something," he tells us. "Ever."

Still, after all these years, you can feel the chip on his shoulder. And that's the way he competed. Pissed off. With a major point to prove. And believe me, Milt Campbell is not the kind of guy you want to piss off. He's got a gut, sure. But he could still twist your head off like a bottle cap. So big was Milt as an athlete that he was told if he got any bigger, he wouldn't be able to run the hurdles. Years later, at twice the size he was when he was told that and long after he'd already won the decathlon gold medal, he ran 13.4 seconds in the 120-yard hurdles to break the world record.

It's absurd that he's not in the Hall of Fame, that his name wasn't even on the ballot when the Olympic Committee chose its first class in 1983. But it's also sort of fitting. I'm amazed by Milt's continual ability to spite the naysayers, to channel all the doubt and disrespect and turn it into his driving fuel. As I sit here listening to him talk, I find myself so captivated that the rest of the room has ceased to exist. It feels like Milt is talking directly to me.

And then, suddenly, he is.

"Dan O'Brien," he says. "Stand up for us, would you please?"

My stomach sinks.

"Go on," he urges.

So I stand up, and the attention in the room turns to me like flowers to the sun.

"Let me ask you something, son," he says. "What do you want?"

"What do I *want*?"

"What do you want," he repeats. "What are your goals? It's a simple question."

He's right. It is a simple question. And I've got the perfect answer.

"I want to be a great athlete," I say confidently.

"That's it? Just a great athlete?"

"Well, yeah. What's wrong with that?"

"There's nothing wrong with it. But if all you want is to be a great athlete, then you might as well go home right now."

"I don't follow."

"Think about it. You're already a great athlete," he says. "You can't go anywhere by being happy with where you're at."

And with that, the room goes stiff. You can feel it. Milt has just made a point that has caught everyone's attention. For the next few minutes, as everyone leans in to listen, he talks about the concept of wanting more, demanding more, expecting more. Instead of resting on the things we have, we need to pursue, with a dogged persistence, the things we don't have. And we have to be specific about what we want, he says. We can't set vague goals like we want to make more money or we want a better life. That's like a tourist in a foreign city telling a cab driver he wants to go downtown. Where downtown? What address? If a man knows where he's trying to go, he can get directions. If he doesn't, he ends up wandering. Something I know a fair amount about.

"Come on, O'Brien," Milt prods. "Tell me, what do you want? Where are you trying to go?"

Suddenly, in this one moment, my entire life's purpose clicks. I don't want to be the next Jackie Joyner-Kersee. I don't want to make the multi-events cool. I don't want to be rich or famous. What I want, I tell Milt, is for people to call me the greatest athlete in the world.

"And how do you plan on making that happen?" he asks.

"By winning the Olympic gold medal."

Milt smiles the smile of a man who has just gotten through to a kid.

"Good," he says. "Now write it down, and don't stop until you get there."

I don't even wait one second. I ask someone for a pen and grab a napkin, and on the front I write: "I will win the Olympic gold medal." Then I flip it over and write: "9,000 points." It's the decathlon's most mythical barrier. Nobody's ever broken it. But I will. This napkin represents a contract with myself. An ironclad commitment. I fold it up and slide it carefully into the back slot of my wallet, and from this day forward, I will carry it with me wherever I go.

I have never been so inspired in all my life.

Coach Sloan, Dan and Coach Keller

Hurdles

They say records are meant to be broken, and for the most part, I agree with this. But the 122 consecutive 400-meter hurdles races that Edwin Moses won between 1977 and 1987, to me, is a record that will never fall. To this day I have a hard time wrapping my head around that number. 122 races. For 10 years he didn't lose to anyone. Anywhere. And this is to say nothing of the unspeakable difficulty of the 400-meter hurdles in the first place. I ran the 300m hurdles in high school and a few 400s in college, and let me tell you, that race is murder. You're so tired at the end of that thing that you might as well be at the end of a boot camp obstacle course. To think that a guy could go that many races without coming in second even one time, without once losing his concentration and clipping a hurdle just a hair too much, without once having an old-fashioned bad day, is insane to me.

I first watched Edwin run in 1984 at the Los Angeles Coliseum when I was competing in the Junior Olympics. He was amazing. I met him a couple times over the years, and I was always struck by his unassuming, soft-spoken nature. It's amazing the animals guys can turn into when the competitive switch flips. Edwin was known for his constant stride pattern, taking exactly 13 steps between each hurdle. Most guys are hitting 14 or 15, and even that's not consistent. But Edwin was a mechanic. An absolute master of efficiency.

122 races? Come on.

Left to right: Harry Marra (coach), Kip Janvrin, Derek Huff, Drew Fucci, Brian Brophy, Sheldon Blockburger, Dave Johnson, Dan O'Brien, Aric Long, Rob Muzzio, Fred Samara (coach)

13

The Visa stipends aren't much, but trust me, everything helps. If you're ranked in the top two, you get $1,000 a month. If you're No. 3 or 4, you get $800. If you're No. 5 or 6, you get $600. And to round it out, Nos. 7 and 8 get $400 and Nos. 9 and 10 get $200. Like I said, it's not a ton. But for me, a thousand bucks would pay my rent almost three times.

Of course, none of us are getting anything yet. We have to wait to see who the top 10 finishers are at the 1991 U.S. Championships in Randall's Island, New York.

But for me, Christmas is about to come early.

"Reebok is interested in signing you," Keller tells me.

"Seriously? For how much?"

"I don't know. But I talked to Jenner, and he put me in touch with George Wallach, the guy who represented him for a long time. He's going to help us negotiate a deal."

I don't know anything about any of this, but OK. That sounds fine. Just get me some money. The Reebok rep is a guy by the name of Chester Wheeler, and we're all meeting at the Best Western in Moscow. Not exactly a New York board room.

"Dan, we really like what we're seeing out of you," Chester says. "We're seeing what you did at the U.S. Championships and the Goodwill Games, and since we just brought Dave Johnson over from Nike, we're thinking we'd like to bring you on board, too."

"I didn't know Dave was with Reebok now."

"Yep."

Chester is pumped about what Reebok's doing. They're trying to keep up with Nike, which he refers to as a "four-letter word." Nike's the Evil Empire, like the Yankees, and I hated the Yankees when I was a kid, so I think it would be pretty cool to join up with the underdog. Reebok's starting to land some pretty big names, with Roger Clemens in their baseball division, Dominique Wilkins for basketball and Rocket Ismail for football, and now they're trying to make a splash in track circles. Chester says that as of right now they don't have a javelin boot or a long jump shoe, but they're going to make Dave and me special pairs. They're going all-in on this fight against Nike, which leaves only one question:

What kind of money are we talking?

I leave while the suits handle the business, and when George comes out he's got a big smile on his face.

"We got you $45,000 a year," he says.

"Holy shit! $45,000!" This sounds like Powerball money to me.

"And we worked a ton of incentives into the deal," he adds. "If you make No. 1 in the world, you get a bonus. If you win the U.S. Championship or World Championship, you get a bonus. Personal bests. American records. World records. Everything gets you more money."

And everything gets Keller more money, too. That's the fine print.

Of the $45,000 I'm getting, 15 of it goes to Keller. That was negotiated without even asking me. Thirty-three percent, to me, seems like a pretty steep price to pay Keller, especially since I'm not paying Sloan a dime. But honestly, I don't feel like I have the right to say anything. I owe this guy. He saved me from drowning, bailed me out of jail, took me in out of the rain that day on his porch. When everyone else in the world had given up on me, he didn't, and $15,000 could never repay him for that.

Besides, I don't have time to worry about that shit.

In February I win the U.S. Indoor Championship in Colorado Springs, scoring 4,321 in the five-event pentathlon. I'm almost unbeatable in a pentathlon, or even a heptathlon for that matter, as neither includes the pole vault or javelin and you only have to run a 1000m instead of a 1500. An 800m is no joke, but it still caters more to speed, and the rest of the events in a pentathlon—60m hurdles, long jump, shot put and high jump—are right in my sweet spot. With the Visa thing and the Reebok deal and this win in Colorado Springs, I feel like I'm riding a monster wave of momentum heading into the U.S. Championships in Randall's Island, New York.

The history at Randall's Island is rich. As the site of the 1936 Olympic Trials, this is where Jesse Owens' quest to win four gold medals at the Berlin Olympics, otherwise known as the Hitler Games, began. Like everyone else, I've become a huge Jesse Owens fan. What this guy did, during the time that he did it, will never be duplicated. A black man winning four gold medals on 1936 German soil with Adolf Hitler in the crowd? Come on. How could you ever top that?

And what makes the story even more incredible is that Owens probably would've lost the long jump without even reaching the finals had it not been for the help of Luz Long, a tall blue-eyed German. As the story goes, Jesse had fouled on his first two passes, and a third foul would've disqualified him. He couldn't get his step right on the new, unfamiliar runway, so Long—who was Germany's best hope to defeat Owens, by the way—walked over to Owens and advised him to adjust his takeoff point, moving it back a few inches from the board just to be safe, as a jumper of Owens' stature could surely spare a couple inches. It seemed impossible that a guy like Luz Long, this classic, blue-eyed model of the master race, would dare help a black opponent right in front of Hitler. But he did. And after accepting the advice and adjusting his step, Jesse went on to make the jump en route to winning his four gold medals.

But that's not even the best part.

After the Olympics, Owens and Long stayed in touch, but eventually and reluctantly, Long was forced into World War II with the German army. Sometime during the war he wrote Owens a letter, and in that letter he made a request: Should he not make it out of the war alive (which he feared he wouldn't), would Owens please go to Germany, find Long's son, and tell him about his father. In 1943 Long was killed in the war, and in 1951 Jesse fulfilled his friend's request by going to Germany and finding Kai Long.

"I've seen Luz again," Jesse was quoted as saying, "in the face of his son."

Now if that doesn't inspire you to run, I don't know what the hell will.

I back into the blocks for the 100-meter, listen for the gun, and bang! I go gangbusters, getting out like a drag car that has timed the light dead-ass perfectly. I run 10.23 seconds.

"Ladies and gentlemen!" the announcer belts out. "A new decathlon world record!"

Holy shit! I just ran 10.23! I thrust my arms in the air, scream at the top of my lungs, and when I look in the stands, Keller and Sloan are doing the same thing. But wait, there's a problem. Apparently, somebody forgot to set up the wind instrument. Every race has to have a wind instrument if the times are to be eligible for records, so even though there's not a breath of wind, my time, on a total technicality, will not go down as the fastest 100m in decathlon history—at least not officially.

But it counts all the same in this meet, and I couldn't be off to a better start.

I parlay my momentum into a long jump of just over 26 feet before throwing just under 53 feet in the shot put. After high jumping 6-foot-9 and running a personal best 47.70 in the 400m, I have ended Day One with a score of 4,747, the highest first-day total ever.

If people weren't talking about me before, they sure as hell are now.

"You just sent a shock wave through the sport," is how Keller puts it.

Frank Zarnowski and current world record holder Daley Thompson are at a track meet in Europe, but when they catch wind of my first day they run straight to the airport and board a plane to New York. At the start of Day Two, you can feel a buzz that wasn't there yesterday, a stirring in the crowd, people shuffling for position when I line up for the hurdles. Suddenly there are two storylines: Is the guy going to break the world record, or is he going to somehow blow this historic first day by letting Dave catch him again? I think a lot of my opponents, not just Dave, are wondering if I'm going to falter, if there's perhaps an outside shot that they could still climb back into this thing.

I think I'm even wondering a little bit.

Clearing Hurdles

To start Day Two I stretch my lead even more by running a personal best 13.95 in the hurdles and throwing a 158-foot discus, another PR. And when it comes time for the pole vault, where everyone's waiting to see how badly I'm going to jump, I shock even myself by going 5-meters-10. Almost 17 feet!

Thanks for coming, fellas. But that's all she wrote.

Keller is completely ecstatic. "That's almost two feet over your Seattle mark!"

But Sloan is more subdued. He just smiles slyly. It's working. It's starting to happen.

"Finish strong," he tells me. "Leave no doubt."

I improve my javelin to 199 feet, and going into the 1500, it's over. Nobody has even a slight chance of catching me. Not Dave. Not anybody. Which is exactly the way I planned it.

Different decathletes have different formulas for winning. Dave Johnson and Bruce Jenner are second-day guys, or more specifically, *late* second-day guys. Dave's a monster javelin thrower, and Bruce's 1500m times are the stuff of decathlon legend. But that will never be my formula. In the mold of the great Daley Thompson, I'm a tailor-made first-day decathlete. A sprinter. A jumper. Coming into this event, my plan was simple: blitz the field through seven events, then maintain my lead through the javelin and pole vault so that in the end, the 1500m doesn't even matter. And I have executed perfectly. I could basically crawl the last half of this race and still win going away.

Of course, there is still the matter of the world record, which is well within reach.

But remember, with no wind instrument on the 100m, it wouldn't be official, anyway.

This is all the excuse I need to throttle back, coming across in 4:36.63 for a score of 8,844, the second highest total in history, just three points behind Daley's 8,847 and more than 200 points better than Bruce Jenner's American record of 8,634. I'll admit, never in my wildest dreams did I think I could come in here and score like that. Nobody saw that coming. Not my coaches. Not my opponents. And especially not Visa. I know this because when I wake up the next morning, I see Dave on the Regis and Kathie Lee show promoting the Visa Decathlon Team alongside Bruce Jenner.

"Son of a bitch," I chuckle to myself.

I can only figure one of two things: Either Visa was so confident Dave would win here in New York that they went ahead and booked him on the show ahead of time, or worse, they think my performance was a fluke, an aberration, and therefore still consider Dave to be the No. 1 guy and the face of the program. I think it's probably the former, but either way, it still irks me. So I stow it away. Athletes will use anything for motivation, and this is classic bulletin-board material.

14

Despite my Regis and Kathie Lee snub, I'm getting loads of attention for this performance. On the night I won, the Visa bigwigs took me out for a fancy Manhattan evening along with the girl I've been dating, Monica, a beautiful Norwegian 800m runner. We did the swanky restaurant and the Broadway play, the whole New York nine, and all night long the Visa guys couldn't stop raving about "the show I put on."

"Unbelievable," they say. "We're so proud of you."

And they are even more proud that the program is working. Whether they expected it or not, the fact remains that in the very first event since Visa signed on as the official sponsor of America's first-ever national decathlon team, one of their athletes threw up the highest score in American history. That's pretty good timing, for if this is all about PR and buzz, then right now track-and-field circles are definitely buzzing.

When I get back to Idaho, I get the new edition of *Track & Field News*. I'm on the cover.

Decathlon Dynamo!
O'Brien Scares 8900

"Get off the tracks," Keller says, almost giddy. "The train's coming."

You're damn right it is.

"By the way," he adds. "I bet you're pretty happy about those incentives right now."

He would be referring to the performance incentives in my Reebok contract, and yes, I'm quite happy. I get five grand for scoring a personal best, 10 grand for breaking the American record, 10 grand for winning the U.S. Championship, and on top of all that, by way of catapulting Dave for the No. 1 American ranking, my Visa stipends have kicked in, so that's another thousand bucks a month. All told I'm suddenly bringing in more than 80 grand, and it's funny how the minute you can finally afford to buy a few things for yourself, the more shit you start getting for free. Reebok is sending me all kinds of stuff. Shoes. Clothes. I'm giving this stuff away like it's Christmas. Coaches. Friends. People I barely even know. If you see a bum walking down the street in Moscow, there's a pretty decent chance he's sporting a brand-new pair of Reeboks.

I also use this newfound money to finally pay off my debt with the university. I write one check for four grand and that's that. The process of putting my past to bed continues.

It all started, I believe, with that very first day I showed up to work with Sloan, that day I waltzed in late and almost left early. That was the day I began moving from the insecure, irresponsible kid I was to the driven, focused athlete I'm starting to become. There was a time when I would've strutted into practice high on the hog after a magazine cover like that, but Sloan's wearing off on me. He says we don't get caught up in that stuff. He says we keep our head down, keep grinding, stick to the routine.

Every day he drums this word into my head. *Routine. Routine. Routine.* And after the results I've seen, I'm not questioning anything he says. I already trust him in a way it takes some athletes years to trust their coach. So when he says there's a guy he wants me to start running with, a guy he thinks can push me to an even higher level, I'm all for it.

"Michael Jobear," he says. "That's your guy."

Michael's a Washington State guy, so I know of him. I've seen him around the track, even talked to him a few times. He's an Australian 400-meter runner who's also training for the world championships, and with piercings and tattoos everywhere, not to mention a Mohawk spiked to a razor's edge, his reputation as a full-blooded crazy man is surely warranted. When I was in college I heard a story about him sneaking onto the track in the middle of the night at the Texas Relays and running a naked 400m.

"He's the toughest little fucker I've ever seen," Sloan says. "He'll run 'til he drops."

You never know how you're going to click with a training partner. It either works or it doesn't. And right away, I know it's going to work with Mick. He's a little tike, 5'5" on a really good day, while I'm a taller, more prototypical runner, and it's that stark physical contrast that helps us bring out the best in each other. If he has to push to keep up with what I can do naturally, I have to find another gear to keep up with what he's willing to do in the way of pure effort.

I'm telling you, the guy is a machine. We'll be running hard 200-meter intervals, 21-22 seconds, and before I've even had time to catch my breath, Mick's up and ready to go again. His recovery rate is insane, almost inhuman for anyone not named Prefontaine, and it's doing exactly what Sloan said it would. Heading into the 1991 World Championships in Tokyo, I'm in the best shape of my life. And on top of that, I'm completely inspired, as about two weeks before I leave I get an envelope in the mail from Bruce Jenner. It's a signed copy of his famous *Sports Illustrated* cover. The message he's written is simple:

"Good luck at worlds. Seize the moment."

Tokyo is another world. Huge skyscraping buildings crammed together like sardines. Neon lights everywhere. Horns honking. Music playing. It's like New York rolled up inside a techno concert. The language barrier is going to be tough, I can tell that right away, but I don't have to understand Japanese to pick right up on how they feel about track and field over here. It's not like America. We don't take a backseat over here. When Jackie Joyner-Kersee steps out onto the sidewalk, people swarm to her.

"Jackie! Jackie!" they yell, holding out pens and paper. "Jackie, over here!"

I stand in the back admiring the way Jackie owns the spotlight, the way she smiles as the flashbulbs pop, waving and signing everything in front of her. Then, in a Japanese accent, somebody yells, "Dan O'Brien!"

Holy shit. They know who I am in Japan?

Jackie quickly grabs me and pulls me in next to her.

"Get used to hearing this guy's name," she says. "He's going to be a star."

I stand there smiling with Jackie as everyone starts snapping pictures. If I wanted to, I could sign autographs for the next five hours. It's crazy how different it is overseas. At home, track athletes are mere stepchildren. But here, Nippon Television, which is like the NBC of Japan, wants to do a documentary on me: "A Day in the Life of Dan O'Brien."

For the next seven days, as I wait for the start of my decathlon, camera crews follow me wherever I go. I quickly hook up with Mick, and together, we start taking the train all over Tokyo, stopping at Electronic City to buy Discmans, snapping pictures at the temple where the Buddhist monks pray. We're like kids in a candy store. I've never been out of America. A few nights before I compete, the TV folks invite me to a traditional Japanese meal, which feels surreal beyond words. Less than three years ago, I was two steps from being a dishwasher at Skippers, and now here I am, taking my shoes off and bowing with some of the highest ranking executives in all of Tokyo.

It's amazing the places running can take you.

During my last year at Idaho, I took a one-unit sports psychology class, the only class I ever actually liked, and we spent a lot of time talking about visualization and positive imagery. In other words, seeing success before it happens. Two days before my decathlon starts I walk around the practice track with Sloan and Keller, and together we go through a mental simulation of every event. I stand in the 100m blocks, getting down in my start position, looking down the runway, seeing myself striding, *bounding*, winning. I do the same from the end of the long-jump runway and inside the shot-put ring, going through my routine exactly as I will in money time. When we get to the high jump, I say to Sloan, "Let me take one jump for real."

"What for? You're ready."

I know I'm ready. That's not what it's about. I'm charged up. I want to jump.

"Come on," I implore. "Just one. Then we can move on."

He sighs. "Fine. One jump."

I end up taking three jumps, and on the last one I clear seven feet.

"That's it," Sloan says, drawing the line. "That's the one to sleep on."

Speaking of sleep, I can't, not a wink, my excitement giving way to the familiar dread of what lies ahead. The totality of the decathlon is always daunting, always intimidating, but even more specifically, it's the close of each day, the hellishly brutal challenge of the 400 and 1500 meters that continues to terrorize my thoughts. Somewhere in the middle of each of those races, there is an inevitable moment of truth, a moment where your whole body is at war with itself, where you're right up against your absolute threshold for pain and exhaustion, and yet, you have to keep going. You have to cross over that line into a place of pure agony. It's an awful place to be, lonely and dark, and no matter how many times you've been there, no matter how many times you've managed to suck it up and fight your way out, the thought of having to go back and do it again never gets any easier. The day before my meet I'm pacing around my room like I'm awaiting the verdict on a death-penalty trial. Sloan and Keller are equally anxious, and so here they go again, cramping my space in the exact moment I need them to back off.

"Remember, stick to the plan in the 400."

OK.

"If it's raining, just go with it. It's the same conditions for everyone."

Got it.

"And if things don't go well early, don't press. It's a long day."

That's the problem.

"Oh and one more thing . . ."

Finally, I have to cut them off. This is making me want to jump out of my skin. I tell them I'm supposed to meet Mick for something to eat, which is a lie, but I have to get the hell out of here. I show up at Mick's room looking frazzled, edgy, and he thinks he's got the perfect remedy: a good-luck haircut. He gets aggressive with the clipper, damn near cleaning my sides to the skin before tapering into a high, almost pointed fade. So now I look like a bullet tip.

I guess I could shave the rest to make it even, but I'm not very big on buzzed heads. And besides, to be perfectly honest, I'm too nervous to give two shits about my hair. That night I toss and turn for three hours before I finally fall asleep, and the next morning I'm no better. I've never been anywhere near an event this big. This makes the U.S. meet at Randall's Island look like a charity walkathon. Next to the Olympics, this is the biggest track meet on the planet. Tonight there'll be almost a hundred thousand people in the stands.

Breathe, Dan. Breathe.

It's at least some comfort that Mick, who doesn't race for a few more days, has come to the practice track to warm up with me. This is something he'll continue to do over the course of my career, as he's quickly figured out that I hate to be alone in these situations. And Mick's nothing but a track rat anyway. Maybe 10 minutes into our stretches, he points to a guy wearing a Japanese headband.

"Hey," he says. "Isn't that that Plaziat clown?"

I look, and indeed it is. Christian Plaziat. Maybe the best French decathlete ever and a notorious loudmouth. A few days ago, he told the press that my score in New York was a fluke, and that there was no way I was going to repeat that performance here in Japan. It reminded me of high school when the kids from Sutherlin were running their mouths.

How'd that work out again?

Coaches aren't allowed on the track or even underneath the stadium, and since Keller and Sloan know I'm a total mess this morning, even worse than usual, they've asked our athletic liaison, Charlie Green, who used to be one of the fastest men in the world, to look out for me as my race nears. He finds me in a hallway bouncing on my toes and taking deep breaths, trying to stay calm.

"Hey man, you doing OK?"

"I'll be all right once we get going (I hope)."

"Listen," Charlie says, "this is no different. Just do what you do. Just run, baby."

The simplicity of the advice snaps me into focus, and with my aerodynamic, bullet-tip do, I get out to a fast start with a 10.41 in the 100m and a 26-foot long jump, and after I throw a personal best 53.28 feet in the shot put, I am once again out to a big lead. I feel completely locked in, completely in control of both the meet and myself. But then, for whatever reason, I lose it in the high jump. Two days ago I went seven feet during my walkthrough with Sloan, but today I barely clear 6-2. By a full six inches it's the worst jump I've taken in the last seven years, and when Michael Smith booms a huge jump of almost seven feet, suddenly, in just one event, my lead has been all but erased. In a decathlon, you can't let up for one second, one event, especially at this level. That's the grind of it.

And so we've arrived at gut-check time. The 400-meter. Cue the nausea.

With a lineup that includes myself, Michael Smith, Christian Plaziat and a Swedish decathlete named Hinrich Daggard, Frank Zarnowski is calling it perhaps the finest 400-meter field in decathlon history. The rain has ceased but the August heat hasn't, a combination that has steam rising from the track like a New York alley. My body is aglow, fully lathered, and my heart is beating like a gong. In this stadium, right now, there are probably 90 thousand people, every one of them standing in anticipation. And yet, you could honestly hear a pin drop. Few things in this world are as electric as the last few seconds before the gun goes off on a big race. The silence is hair-raising.

The call goes out.

"On your mark."

Breathe, Dan. Breathe.

"Set . . . Bang!"

I get out clean and find my stride fast, and immediately fall into my rhythm. The 400-meter is the longest short race in track. If you go out too soon, you're dead. You'll never hang on. But at the same time, hanging back even a hair of a second too long is equally suicidal. I want to be at 200 meters at precisely 22 seconds, 300 meters at 33 seconds, and then kick home with whatever I have left. This is the strategy. The plan. But then, every runner has a plan.

The problem is actually sticking to it.

At 100 meters, a few guys start to go, start to break away a little bit, and this is where plans tend to blow up. You're charged up on adrenaline because 90 thousand people are screaming and because you're scared to death of losing, and you simply don't have the discipline to remain patient. The racer's instinct is strong. When I feel this first group start to break off, it takes every ounce of restraint I have to let them go. I couldn't do it if I didn't harbor an absolute trust for my training, if I didn't believe wholeheartedly in my coaches, if I wasn't 100 percent committed to the plan. But I *do* trust my training. I *do* believe in my coaches. I *am* committed to the plan.

I hit 170 meters, 180 meters, 190 meters, and now I start to go. At 200 meters I start gliding past guys like they've got the brakes on, like a racehorse making his move, and just like that I've moved into the lead. By 300 meters I've broken completely free, and as I round the final turn and move onto the homestretch, as I hit the point in the race where the bear normally jumps on my back, where my muscles normally flood with lactic acid, somehow, I'm actually getting stronger, a mere two months with Mick having turned me into a fucking machine. Ninety thousand people are on their feet cheering, but I swear I can hear Sloan and Keller yelling, "Go to the arms! Kick, Danny boy! Kick!" I drop the clutch and go, tapping into a gear I didn't even know I had, powering through the final 70 meters to cross in a lightning-fast time of 46.53, my personal best by more than a full second.

I throw my arms high in the air, as though breaking through a ribbon, as the stadium erupts in cheer. They know their track in Japan, so it's not lost on them how fast 46.53 is for a decathlete. It's a monster time, good enough to completely blast what was, perhaps, the best 400-meter decathlon field ever assembled. This is by far and away the biggest moment of my life to this point. In front of 90 thousand people, I've made a statement not only to the rest of the decathlon world, but maybe more importantly, to myself. *I can do this. I can honestly be the best in the world.* At the first place Keller and Sloan are allowed, they come barreling down the hall and almost tackle me.

"Holy shit!" Sloan shouts. "That was beautiful!"

Perfection, they say, is unattainable. But this was about as close to a perfect race as I could've possibly run. We're on cloud nine, a moment frozen in time as we all stand in the hallway, smiling, looking at each other. We just stepped onto the biggest stage and put on a show. We're excited, even ecstatic, and we're more determined than ever. Keller says what we're all thinking.

"It's ours to lose now."

It's the start of Day Two, 9:30 in the morning, and the Tokyo skies have opened up to a torrential downpour. It's an excuse if you want it, and believe me, there are a lot of decathletes looking for an excuse—an injury that's not quite as bad as they're making it look, a deficit that's too big to even try to erase, any reason at all to bail out just that little bit, if only mentally, because this event is just so damn taxing.

If I'm being honest, I gave myself an out in Norwalk when I conceded that Dave was going to beat me. I didn't want to run that 1500. I wasn't fooling anyone. So I reasoned that Dave's lead was simply too big to overcome, thus allowing myself a built-in escape clause when push came to shove. But today I will allow myself no such excuse. That 400-meter changed something in me. Today, I will make the same commitment that Carl made at the '88 Trials when he jumped almost 29 feet in a storm that was bordering on biblical.

Nothing beats me today. Nothing gets in my way.

While the other athletes stay beneath cover until the very last second, I walk onto the track a full five minutes before the start of the high hurdles. I stand at the start line and let the rain pour over me, accepting it in a way that I actually begin to like, as though I'm taking God's best shot and smiling. The more drenched I get, the stronger I feel.

"Today," I whisper to myself, "I become a world champion."

I send a quick and clear message by running 13.94 in the hurdles, making me the only guy to break 14 seconds. Then I throw an easy 155-foot discus, the third-highest mark behind Michael Smith's 159 and Spanish sensation Antonio Penalver's 166. These first two events of Day Two are quickly becoming legitimate strengths of mine—my discus prowess, much like my shot put, belying my more slender sprinter's frame.

When it comes time to pole-vault, the stadium is bare due to the afternoon change over, and any apprehension, any fear

After the Tokyo vault

I've ever harbored for this event, has gone right out the window, my jittery adrenaline superseding every other emotion. I start down the runway without an ounce of hesitation, planting the pole with confidence, conviction, commitment, allowing the physics to take over as I clear a clean 5-meters-20, over 17 feet. And in that one jump, I have just taken the decathlon, quite literally, to another level. Guys who can run and jump like me don't usually pole-vault over five meters or throw the discus close to 160 feet. If I've already established myself as the best first-day decathlete in the world, if not the best ever, then what does it say that in one year of working with Sloan I've gone from a downright atrocious pole-vaulter to putting up the highest mark of any decathlete in the eight-year history of the World Championships?

I am a champion!

If this is the way it's going to be, how will anyone beat me?

I throw the javelin a personal best 199 feet to again move within striking distance of the world record. I want it. I think I can run the 4:32 I need to get it. But in the end, I fall just short, going 4:37.50—which is actually the second-best time of my life—for a final score of 8,812, making me the new American record holder and the first decathlete in history to surpass 8,800 points twice in the same year.

Oh, and in case you were wondering about Plaziat, he finished at 8,122. Ninth place.

If he's still talking, nobody's listening.

Discus

For most people's money, mine included, Carl Lewis is the single greatest American Olympian of all time. For both his dominance and significance, you have to throw Jesse Owens in that conversation, as well. Michael Johnson. Michael Phelps. Mark Spitz. Jackie Joyner-Kersee. Edwin Moses. The list of great American Olympians is as long as it is proud. But the one you might never have heard of, the one who probably flies the farthest under the radar, is the great discus thrower Al Oerter.

I heard him speak at one of the earliest Visa Clinics, and his story blew me away.

For starters, he's one of only two athletes in history, the other being Carl Lewis, to win a gold medal at four successive Olympics. His first came in 1956 at the Melbourne Games. Then it was Rome in 1960, Tokyo in 1964, and finally, Mexico City in 1968. Even more impressive, he broke the Olympic record all four times, something nobody else has done.

Now you would think that a guy who wins four straight gold medals would be heads and tails better than anyone else in the world, but never once was Al the actual favorite to win. In fact, he never even won the Olympic trials. A couple times he had to scrape to even make the team. But in the words of the great triple jumper Mike Conley, who once told me "it only takes one jump to be the best in the world," Al's legacy lies in his amazing ability to stay entirely in the moment, to rise to the occasion, to summon his finest performance when he needed it most, despite facing what most would consider to be insurmountable adversity.

Consider that shortly after Al won his first gold medal at the age of 20, in 1957, he nearly died in a car accident. People said his career was over. But Al had other plans, going to Rome in 1960 and throwing 194 feet, 2 inches to break his own Olympic record. Then, just days before he was set to defend his title at the '64 Games in Tokyo, he tore the cartilage from his ribcage. Anyone who has ever suffered an injury to that area knows that it's hard enough to breathe, let alone throw the discus. Doctors told him to pull out of the competition and begin a six-week recovery. Instead, Al threw 200 feet, 1 inch to break his third Olympic record. And of course, in 1968, they said his time was over. In 1956 he was too young, and now in 1968 he was too old. It was always something. But Al, as usual, didn't pay a second's worth of attention to any of the skeptics. He simply stepped into the ring and threw 212 feet, 6 inches for his fourth gold medal. He probably would've won a fifth, too, as in 1980 he threw over 227 feet, but America boycotted the Olympics.

Incredible.

When I heard Al tell this story, I couldn't believe my ears.

And he was so self-deprecating about the whole thing. No ego whatsoever. He told his story because people wanted him to, but he was clearly more interested in other people's stories. You could tell he didn't think he was anything special—just a guy who threw the discus a few times, a guy who now paints for a living, a guy who once joked, without an ounce of bitterness: "I don't think the discus will ever attract any attention until they let us start throwing them at each other."

That's Al. Funny and humble. And the greatest Olympian a lot of people don't know.

15

I'm in Atlanta for the fall Visa clinic, and I've arrived to nothing but handshakes and high-fives. Rafer. Milt. Mathias. Toomey. They're all patting me on the back for winning the world title, for breaking Jenner's 15-year-old record, for becoming the No. 1-ranked decathlete in the world in just my second year as a pro. They're not quite welcoming me into their exclusive fraternity, for the exclusivity, of course, rightly lies in the gold medal. But they see me. They recognize what I'm doing. And given the nice note he sent me before Tokyo, I'm expecting Jenner to be equally complimentary.

But as I'm about to find out, that's just not Bruce's way.

I don't know a lot about Bruce at this point, but over the years I will come to learn that like a lot of great champions, he's prizefighter proud. A competitor to the core. And when I look back, it will be this night in Atlanta where I got my first taste of this mentality—the night when he made no mention of the fact that I broke his American record, but instead, he criticizes my 1500-meters and goes on to compare our running events side by side.

"So I added up our running totals," he says, "and I actually scored higher than you."

He hands me the score sheet as proof.

"Here," he says. "Have a look."

To say this has caught me off guard would be an understatement. I don't even know what to say. I find it hard to believe that his running totals are actually higher than mine.

Dan and Bruce Jenner

How can that be possible when I outscored him by more than 200 points? I take a closer look at the sheet, and to my sincere surprise, it's true. Bruce's running total is indeed higher than mine.

It's worth mentioning that this is merely a product of the 1500m (where his times, on average, are a good 30-40 seconds, and thus, some 200 points better than mine), as my times in each of the other three running events are far superior to his. But still, in the end, what he's saying is true. His running total, technically, is higher than mine.

"We have to get you running that 1500-meter better," he says.

Though he doesn't make the offer directly to me, Bruce has suggested to my coaches that I move down to Los Angeles where he can oversee my training. Says I can work out at Pepperdine University. Bruce is known for the way he trained, for the way he basically taught himself, with no real coach, basing himself out of San Jose but traveling around to different tracks to work with different single-event specialists. One day he'd go with the long jumpers. Another day he'd do work with sprinters or vaulters. He believes this is the right way to do it, to break away from your comfort zone and stretch your limits. And for him, obviously, it worked.

But I'm not Bruce. He's a great champion, and I'm flattered he wants to work with me, but with all due respect, wild horses couldn't drag me away from Sloan and Keller right now. We've got a great thing going. We just won the world championship. We just broke the American record and damn near the world record. And this is to say nothing of the immense loyalty they've shown me, especially Keller, without whom who knows where I would be. To leave now? After everything he's done for me? Like I said, it's a flattering offer. But I'm not going anywhere.

The Reebok corporate convention takes me to Orlando, Florida, in the fall of 1991. They're putting everyone up in a plush Disney World hotel—the athletes, the big execs, and it's really cool to feel like a part of the team. Everywhere I go, people are coming up to me and shaking my hand, asking if they can grab a quick picture.

"We're so glad to have you on board," they tell me. "We've got big plans for you."

They're not kidding.

A few days later, as the convention is drawing to a close, Dave and I get wind that the marketing people want to take a meeting with us, and suddenly our agents are in town.

"You have any idea what this is about?" Dave asks me.

"Nope. You?"

"Nope."

Next thing we know, we're sitting in a conference room with a group of bigwigs. They flip off the lights and turn on an overhead projector, and the presentation begins.

"We've got an idea," the guy says with a huge smile. "Dan or Dave."

Dan or Dave?

"Dan or Dave," he repeats proudly. "Who is the world's greatest athlete?"

These guys can hardly contain their excitement, like they're sitting on the next big thing, but Dave and I still aren't really sure what they're talking about. So they explain further, and it goes like this: With Dave and I being the No. 1- and No. 2-ranked American decathletes, and therefore representing America's two best hopes to bring back a gold from the 1992 Barcelona Olympics, Reebok wants to develop a series of commercials featuring the two of us. In these commercials, we will be pitted against one another, lifting weights, running and jumping, doing all sorts of things on opposite sides of a split screen as a voiceover asks the question: Who is the world's greatest athlete? Dan or Dave? To be settled in Barcelona.

"This is going to be big," they say.

Again, they're not kidding. They're sinking 25 million bucks into this thing. Planning to debut the commercials during the Super Bowl. Right now the only sports marketing campaigns that could even compare would be Nike's Spike Lee and Michael Jordan commercials ("It's gotta be the shoes, money!") and the "Bo Knows" series, and maybe Andre Agassi's "Image is Everything" with Canon cameras. But from what they're telling us, even those pale in comparison to the sheer scale and scope of this idea, which has been organized by the biggest ad agency in New York, the same place that did the Energizer Bunny.

"If you guys are on board, we want to announce this thing later today."

Dave and I both agree that this sounds awesome, but there's only one problem: Neither of us has actually qualified for the Olympic team yet. Sure, we're the top two guys, heads and tails better than any other American, but still, nothing's set in stone. We still have to finish in the top three at next year's U.S. Championships (U.S. Olympic trials), and on any given day, anything can happen.

But Reebok is very clear.

"That's a chance we're more than willing to take."

So there we are, Dave and I, standing in the hallway of this giant auditorium. Inside are about a thousand people, corporate hot shots and the like, and we can hear the commotion bellowing. It's one of those company morale events, somebody up on stage is trying to get everyone fired up. Finally we hear the speaker say, "And now, we have a big treat."

He goes through the whole spiel, telling everyone what the campaign is all about, and you can hear everyone getting excited. "Ladies and gentlemen," he shouts, "let's give a big Reebok welcome to Dan and Dave!"

And just like that, Dave and I are running through a set of swinging saloon doors into a raucous auditorium, everyone cheering and high-fiving us as we make our way toward the stage like we're the next contestants on "The Price is Right." They're really rolling out the red carpet for us. We feel like a big deal, like real-life celebrities.

We don't know it yet, but our lives will never be the same.

The first thing I learn in shooting these commercials is that I never want to be an actor. The schedule is crazy: 5 a.m. call times, 12-hour days, and hours of sitting around waiting for the right lighting. We're shooting at the Los Angeles Coliseum, where I raced in the Junior Olympics all those years ago. I didn't know Dave was at that same event.

"I was still in college," he tells me. "That was my first Olympic trials. 1984."

All the downtime on set is giving Dave and me a chance to get to know each other, and I'm discovering that we have a lot more in common than our Oregon roots and similar-sounding names. Dave, like me, doesn't come from a big prestigious track program. He went to an NAIA college in Los Angeles called Azusa Pacific, and even more similar to me, he may never have tried the decathlon had it not been for the urging of one of his earliest coaches—a coach who, coincidentally, saw him three-step hurdle on his very first attempt.

Dave also has a history with drinking. Both his parents were alcoholics. And Dave was pretty heavy into the booze when he was younger, as well. Come to find out, he didn't actually move to Oregon until his senior year in high school. Before that he was in Montana, where he was getting into all sorts of trouble. Breaking into houses. Running from the cops.

"I was in a bad stretch," he says.

You think?

"But then I turned my life over to Christ."

I grew up going to church, I tell Dave I am certainly a believer but don't attend regularly. But anything that gets a man to change his life for the better, I have to respect. Dave says he was at football practice during his senior year of high school when one of the other wide receivers started talking to him about the Lord. Something clicked. And now here he is, a world-class athlete and one of the best people you could ever know. I've said it before, and I'll say it again: Dave Johnson is as nice a guy, as genuine a guy, as you're ever going to find in this world.

But I'm still going to beat him in Barcelona.

Why? Because Reebok gave me this special shoe. The Pump.

This is my line for the latest commercial we're shooting. In it, I'm opening a box of the new Reebok Pumps while looking over my shoulder and whispering like the whole thing's on the hush, like Reebok is secretly trying to help me beat Dave by giving me this new shoe. Meanwhile, they keep cutting back to Dave, who's doing and saying the same thing on what appears to be an entirely different track, even though I'm standing behind the camera watching him do his takes. "Reebok wants *me* to win," he says, looking over his shoulder. "That's why they gave me this special shoe. The Pump."

Then he laughs like he's really pulling a fast one and says, "But don't tell Dan."

Then I laugh and say, "But don't tell Dave."

Then boom, the Reebok logo slams hard and it says, "To be settled in Barcelona."

Over the years, the commercials will become more and more cheesy to look back on, but right now, at the time, we are the shit. We're one of the first through the new-age sports-marketing wall. We're trying things out. Seeing what works. Ad-libbing and having fun with the whole thing. We end up shooting all over Los Angeles, but for the final commercial we don't have to do anything. Instead, they've rounded up some photos and home-video footage of Dave and me when we were kids—Dave riding his bike and swimming in the lake, me running around the backyard at three years old with a cowboy hat on—perhaps to imply that we've been on a collision course long before we ever knew it, or even that one of us was predestined to be the greatest athlete in the world.

This is the one that's going to debut during the Super Bowl.

I order a 12-foot sub and buy a ton of beer and invite a big group of people over to my townhouse to watch the game. It's the Redskins against the Bills, and somewhere in the first quarter the commercial comes on, the dramatic music, little Dave and me side by side, my brownish-blond hair, just as I remember it, as curly as a pig's tail.

"It's on!" somebody yells. "Everyone be quiet!"

Drum roll . . . .

Dan can run the 100-meter in 10.3 seconds.

Dave can throw the javelin 236 feet.

Dan won the decathlon at the world championships.

Dave won the decathlon at the Goodwill Games.

This summer they'll battle it out in Barcelona for the title of World's Greatest Athlete.

Everyone erupts.

"Awesome, man! Fuckin' awesome!"

To see myself on television is like an out-of-body experience, truly strange, but in the end, this isn't a day for just Dave and me. This is a day for the entire decathlon fraternity. Never has our sport been front and center like this, on hundreds of millions of televisions on Super Bowl Sunday. I think about Milt and Rafer, Jenner and Toomey, and the man who started it all, Jim Thorpe. I think about Frank Zarnowski sitting in those hotel rooms with Fred Samara and Harry Marra, the three of them racking their brains trying to figure a way to put the decathlon on the mainstream map. Well, here we are. Finally.

"Dude," one of my friends says, "you're going to be a star."

I'm excited and surrounded by booze, a dangerous combination, my party instincts kicking into overdrive. I crank my new sound system up as loud it will go, and though the commercials air a few more times during the game, I don't see any of them. I'm too busy playing quarters and hanging out with my boys.

I'm pretty well lit up by the third quarter.

When your life changes, there's no warning. It just happens. One day I'm a virtually unknown athlete, at least outside track-and-field circles, and then, in one 30-second clip, I'm a celebrity. Dave and I are on billboards all over the country. Suddenly I've got endorsement deals with Ray-Ban sunglasses and Tag Heuer. I'm doing Ralph Lauren photo shoots and celebrity appearances for 10 grand a pop. *People Magazine* has named me one of its 50 Most Beautiful People, so now it takes me an hour to run to the grocery store because I'm signing a hundred autographs in the parking lot. People know where I live. They wait outside. Sometimes a dozen or more, snapping pictures.

It never fails that someone shouts, "Hey, where's Dave?"

It's like people think we're brothers or something, or maybe they just want it to be that way. "Dan and Dave" has struck a chord, as things will do from time to time, and the whole thing, really, is starting to get pretty crazy. We show up at the Modesto Relays, a central California meet that never attracts more than a few thousand fans, and suddenly this tiny stadium is jam-packed with 20 thousand people, fans screaming and reaching across the rope trying to grab at us like we're the friggin' Beatles. When two policemen have to intervene and usher us through, pushing people back, Dave looks at me and says, "This is insane."

Yeah, you could say that.

I come to Modesto because it's a great place to get some good last-minute competition, but this year it is damn near impossible. I try to find some privacy in the massage tent with Brian Tibbitts, whom I've started working with. Brian's a massage therapist with Eastern Washington University, and we're growing pretty close pretty fast. He's a bearded, easy-going dude with a ponytail, about six feet tall and pretty stout. We call him Bear. I like him because he doesn't try to talk to me about track. With Bear, it's all about bullshit, nothing heavy, because Bear doesn't do heavy. Bear's the kind of guy you could see sitting around a campfire passing a joint and strumming a guitar, so laid back that sometimes you want to check for a pulse, and that rubs off on me. Just to be around him instantly helps me relax. As he's rubbing down my back, we see a hand slide underneath the tent.

"What the hell?" he says.

Then we see another hand.

"Dude, I think somebody's trying to steal your bag."

It's true. Two kids hatched a plan to sneak into the tent and grab my gear, so now I've got two security guards with me wherever I go. All Bear and I can do is laugh. Crazy.

If I grew up in a house where it was hard to get a lot of attention, then I'm definitely making up for lost time. I run the hurdles and win, sign autographs until my hand cramps, then head out to the booth where my dad is selling the pictures he's drawn of me. He's proud as hell of what I'm doing, and of his own talents, and these pictures are a reflection of both. The details are stunning. Right down to the gap in my teeth, he's captured every nuance of me in the most classic track poses. The coiled discus thrower. The hurdler in midair. My personal favorite, though, is the one where I'm throwing a javelin. He calls it the warrior.

When I snap a photo with a guy who's just bought three different pictures, he says to me, "I'm definitely a Dan guy."

I'm sure Dave's getting the same thing, people telling him they're *Dave* guys, which is exactly what Reebok wanted. The public is choosing sides, proudly announcing whose corner they'll be in come Olympic time, and it's creating a buzz unlike anything track and field has ever seen. Personally, I'm loving it. It's hectic, sure, but this is a whirlwind. One night we get the VIP treatment at the Lakers game, courtside seats at the Forum.

"Ladies and gentlemen," they announce. "Dan and Dave are in the house!"

The whole place stands and cheers. Including Jack Nicholson! This is bizarre!

After I win my second consecutive U.S. Indoor title, scoring 4,497 in the pentathlon at the Kibbie Dome, I go to the Sunkist

Invitational at the Los Angeles Sports Arena and win another pentathlon. Afterward, I do an interview with Maria Shriver, who has her own sit-down show on NBC.

It starts off harmless enough: "Today we're with Dan O'Brien," and so on. But then it goes south. Quickly. Before I know it I'm being asked about my adoption and if it was hard growing up the way I did, which is something I've never talked about with anyone, let alone on national television. Then Maria turns the page to my drinking and my failing out of school and every other negative thing about my apparently scathing life. I don't even know what I'm giving for answers. I'm so uncomfortable, so caught off guard by these questions that I'm simply saying whatever I can to move the hell on. I'm too scared to even watch the interview when it airs, but Keller does, and he's pissed. Says they ran my DUI mug shot.

"That was the worst press possible!" Keller yells. "Jesus!"

"I know. I don't even know what happened."

"Didn't they tell you what they were going to ask?"

"Hell no. I thought it was just going to be a regular interview."

"Son of a bitch," he says, stewing. "They ambushed you."

Ah, the flipside of fame.

16

The 1992 U.S. Track and Field Championships, which double as the Olympic trials, are being held at Tad Gormley Stadium in New Orleans. In the heart of July, it's the kind of hot only people from the South can understand—over 100 degrees and swampy humid. Sloan is obsessing about dehydration. The minute we get to the hotel he finds two five-gallon jugs and fills them up with half Gatorade, half water.

"Drink this," he says, handing me a plastic cup. "Drink as much as you can hold."

A few days before the decathlon we head to the track for our normal walk-through, and somehow, I think it's gotten even hotter. This place is like hell's waiting room. Off to the side of the track are two air-conditioned medic tents, and come tomorrow, Sloan says, they're going to be the busiest places in New Orleans.

"Guys are going to be dropping like flies in this heat," he says. "Cramps. Dehydration. You name it." Then he turns to me. "You been drinking that mix I made?"

"Are you kidding? I'm going to be pissing fruit punch for a year."

"Good," he says, his face straight. "We'll get some more in you when we get back."

He's starting to get antsy, and I'm not far behind.

Earlier this year Visa held a clinic at this very stadium for the sole purpose of giving us a chance to familiarize ourselves with the place, get a feel for the runways and the surface and just the general surroundings. It's a comfort thing, like a golfer not wanting to go into the Masters never having stood on the first tee. You want your eyes to be adjusted to everything. Where's the scoreboard? What's in my peripheral vision from the high-jump pit? I feel pretty comfortable with everything in my walk-through, but then we get to the pole-vault area.

"What's the problem?" Sloan asks, noticing me checking things out pretty hard.

"It's nothing. I've just never vaulted here."

Back at that Visa clinic, just as I was about to get in a few practice vaults, I was asked to do a short appearance with Jenner.

"There's a group of kids over at an elementary school who'd love to hear your story."

Listen, I have no problem talking to kids, but now, while everyone else is getting their work in on the track, I'm not. So here I am, one day from the biggest meet of my life, and I've never vaulted in this stadium. Should it be that much different from any other pit? Probably not.

But it's just one more thing to think about.

My family rolls in about the same time as my nerves, a day out, and it's only making things worse on my stomach that I've flooded with fluid. Sloan is pumping this stuff into me like he's trying to put out a fire. "More," he says. "Get some more in you."

"I can't drink any more."

"Yes, you can. Come on, bottoms up."

The next morning I can't stop pacing, fidgeting, going to the bathroom. My bladder is full and nervous, much like my head, where a thousand thoughts are bouncing back and forth like a pinball machine. Per my routine, I try to run it out on the practice track, but as I make my way into the stadium, the relentless sun already bearing down, a fresh wave of anxiety comes charging in when I feel the electric energy of the crowd.

This place is buzzing, and it's not because Carl Lewis and Michael Johnson and Mike Powell are here. I think back to my first U.S. Championships in Norwalk, where guys were making cracks about someone's family having shown up, the fan count no more than a few hundred for the decathlon. Today I bet there are 30 thousand people, maybe more, crammed into a stadium that seats 25—half of them in bright red shirts, the other half in blue. I wonder, what's the deal with the shirts?

When I get closer, I realize that the red shirts say *Dan* while the blue shirts say *Dave*.

Dave looks at me, "Wow. This is going to be interesting."

That would be one word for it.

When I make my way onto the track, you can literally feel the crowd stirring. People are pointing, popping pictures, and pretty soon the chants start up.

"Dan! Dan! Dan!"

Then another group.

"Dave! Dave! Dave!"

I blow out all my nervous energy by running a quick sprint right along the stands, like a racecar burning out to give the fans a thrill. Everyone cheers, and my adrenaline goes through the roof. I have to calm down. Focus. I tell myself: Forget about

Dan and Dave

all this hoopla and concentrate on the task at hand. Win the U.S. title. Make the Olympic team. That's it.

After Day One, I'm well in line to do both.

Once again, I have raced out to a huge lead. I go 10.5 in the 100m, 25-9 in the long jump, 54-5 in the shot put (which is fast becoming one of my better events), 6-8 in the high jump, and 47.92 in the 400-meter, after which I am so dehydrated and hot that I feel like I'm going to faint, my knees weak and my head spinning. I can only imagine what it would be like had I not dumped about 20 gallons of waterade into my body over the last three days.

I start off Day Two with a 14.23 in the hurdles and a 157-foot discus.

"You're on world-record pace," Keller informs me.

So here we are at the pole vault, and as I stare down the runway in preparation for my first attempt, my mind is totally clear. The way the pole vault works is simple: The bar can only go up, never down. They start it low and bump it up incrementally, and more times than not guys will take their first jump at a pretty easy height just to get a mark under their belt. I decide I'm going to wait until the bar reaches 4 meters 80—or 15 feet, 9 inches—to take my first jump. It's a pretty high bar at which to take my first jump, but that's what I start at every day in practice, and Coach Sloan has quickly molded me into a model of routine.

"We practice the same way we compete," he preaches. "And vice versa."

I will believe in this philosophy until the day I die, this idea of an athlete doing things in the game the same way he does them in practice, but it only works if you do things in practice the way you do them in the game. And I do. Sloan makes me. When I pole-vault on the track in Pullman, I make it like I'm at the world championships, like everything is on the line, and every time I set my opening height at 4 meters 80. And I clear it with my eyes closed.

If there's a flaw in this decision, it's probably not so much the height as it is how long I now have to wait for the bar to get there. A lot of guys are taking a lot of jumps at lower heights, which leaves me sitting around in the sun. I should be up and moving, staying loose, but it's so hot that I don't want to waste any energy. I go under the stadium to find some shade, and I wait and wait, and after an hour, maybe more, my time finally comes. I charge down the runway with a clear mind, but when I stick the pole, for whatever reason, I ease up, just like I used to do before Sloan got a hold of me, absolutely no penetration, and as a result I go straight up and straight back down. The crowd groans.

That's one.

The rule with the pole vault, as with the long jump, high jump, discus and shot put, is three fouls and you're out. If you don't have a mark by your third foul, you don't get any points for that event. Now someone like me can probably overcome a low height because I'm so far ahead in points, but nobody can overcome a no-height. To score zero points in any one event, at this level, is basically decathlon death. I know it. Everyone knows it. So after I foul, you can feel just the slightest bit of tension enter the stadium. But I'm still not nervous. I don't know what happened on that jump, but all I need to do is regroup and make this next one. No big deal.

I start down the runway, and this time I get great penetration, driving through the pole and lifting easily. I'm over clean and on my way down when, at the last second, the very tip of my shoe clips the bar ever so slightly. But it's enough. The bar wiggles and falls, and suddenly things have gotten very serious. To foul once is one thing, but when a guy is down to his last jump, anything can happen. You never want to let it get this far, but it has, and the tension now is as stiff as a board. Everyone in this stadium, and everyone at home watching on TV, is thinking the same exact thing: If Dan doesn't make this height, the best decathlete in the world, the guy who was on world-record pace five minutes ago, the co-star of this bigger-than-life advertising campaign, isn't even going to make the Olympic team.

I'm determined to be the only one *not* thinking this.

Bruce Lee says that the fighter who thinks about dying is already dead, so I try to clear my mind, try to erase the thought of what has happened and concentrate on what I have to do on this jump, try to block out the consequences of missing this jump. But it's nearly impossible. The pressure is like nothing I could've ever imagined, almost to the point of being paralyzing.

I think, *How did I let it get here?*

Then I think, *No! It doesn't matter how I got here! I'm here all the same. Right now, I need to concentrate. Penetration. Hands high. Just like in practice.*

I take a deep breath and start down the runway, but no, something feels off, so I stop.

"Oooohhh!" the crowd moans, their teeth clenching as if they just averted a car wreck.

And now the tension is razor sharp, because the clock is ticking like the final grains of sand in an hourglass. You only get two minutes between jumps, so now I'm rushed, even a little panicked. I can hear the crowd shuffling nervously, jockeying for position, every last eye bearing down on me with the weight of the world, every camera zooming in as my heart beats like a drum.

Come on, Dan. One jump.

I take off down the shoot, no turning back now, but the instant I lift off I know I'm not going to make it, and it's the worst, most helpless feeling I've ever felt. It's like I'm suspended in midair, everything happening in slow motion, and I'm telling myself, "Just get over. Do anything to get over." But I can't. It's like that dream where you want to run but your legs weigh a thousand pounds. I just can't lift, can't go any higher, and as I sail under the bar and fall flat against the mat, an eerie hush falls over not only Tad Gormley Stadium, but over the entire track-and-field world.

Dan O'Brien just no-heighted.

The No. 1 decathlete in the world is out of the Olympics.

Clearing Hurdles

Word circulates like wildfire, and before I even have a chance to catch my breath, I've got people coming up to me from every direction, patting me on the back, telling me it's OK, but I'm in such a state of shock that I can't even hear them. It's like I'm outside my own body, the weirdest feeling you could ever imagine, and all I can think is *This can't be happening. This has to be a dream.*

I walk around in a fog, looking back at the pit with bewilderment, and when I finally start coming to a little bit, Dave is one of the first guys to come up to me and give me a hug.

"Keep your chin up," he whispers in my ear. "Your time will come."

As this whole Dan and Dave thing played out, people got the impression that we were friends rather than competitors, but in the end, we were both out here trying to beat each other. Still, I know Dave is genuine. I know he's hurting for me. As is Bear, who always knows what to say, but at the moment can't find the words. Keller and Sloan find me, and as we try to get away from the track and find some privacy, about six camera crews follow us. Flashbulbs are popping, and I'm looking at the ground like a shamed celebrity who's getting taken away in handcuffs, my coaches by my side telling everyone to please give us some space.

Keller is distraught but he's doing his best.

Sloan, on the other hand, is almost inconsolable. I think, in some small way, he feels a little bit guilty for this. After all, he's my pole-vault coach. He's the one who had me set the bar that high. To be clear, I would never in a million years blame him for this. I'm the one who missed the jump. But a man feels what he feels, and I think Sloan's being pretty hard on himself right now.

"How could this happen?" he says. "I just don't understand."

Nobody does.

As we make our way back through the media swarm and up to the Visa suite, I start to come out of my fog. The reality that I've just blown my shot at the Olympics is beginning to sink in. When I get inside the suite, the first person I see is my mom, and when I put my head on her shoulder and she says, "I'm sorry, sweetheart," all my emotions hit me at once. For the next five minutes I cry like a baby, everything spilling out. And when I'm done, strangely, I feel relieved. Refreshed. Everyone would understand if I pulled out of the final two events, but my coaches and I want to do the right thing. I want to show people that I'm strong enough to finish, that while I might be a lot of things, a quitter is not one of them. I throw a pretty nice javelin and run a surprisingly painless, pressure-free 1500-meter to finish with a score of 7,856—good enough for 11th place.

Dave wins easily after putting together the best second-day performance in decathlon history, 4,455, while Aric Long and Rob Muzzio round out the top three to make up the 1992 United States Olympic decathlon team. I stand at the line and congratulate them all. This is their day, not mine—though not really.

The truth is, for the rest of time, nobody will ever talk about the 1992 Olympic trials for who won. They'll talk about it for who lost. Over the next few days, I will come to learn that nearly every major news network in the country led off their broadcast not with the recent launch of the Columbia space shuttle, not with the strongest earthquake to hit the United States in 40 years, not even with the recent indictments handed down in the Iran-Contra Affair, one of the biggest political scandals ever. Instead, they led with me. Within five minutes, the shot of me flying under that bar was circulating the world. People were already calling it "the most shocking moment in U.S. Olympic history."

It's a tough pill to swallow that I set the bar at almost 16 feet when anything over 12 would've gotten me on the team. But having said that, if anyone thinks this might be it for me, that this might be the end of Dan O'Brien, they've got another thing coming. I will learn from this. I swear on everything holy that I will use it as motivation to be better than I've ever been. As I tell *Good Morning America* the following day, I will be back. You can count on that.

And in the meantime, I'm going to try to forget this ever happened.

For the next few days, I proceed to tear down Bourbon Street. I'm hammered for 48 straight hours. Hell, 20 minutes before I did that *Good Morning America* interview I was stumbling in from the bar, my eyes squinting in the morning light. For the life of me I just can't stop thinking that somehow this isn't real, that somehow, somebody is going to do something to put me on the team. Just minutes after I missed my final vault, Tanja Bufford, a fantastic 400-meter hurdler, came up to me and said, "They're not going to let this stand. This is exactly what we needed to happen for them to finally step up and make a change."

The change, pretty simply, would be to stop determining the members of the Olympic team based solely on the results of one single meet. Every elite athlete would be in favor of this change, as under the current qualifying format it's the elite athletes who are put at the most risk. If you're No. 1 in the world, if you're Carl Lewis or Jackie Joyner-Kersee, you have absolutely nothing to gain at the trials and everything to lose. If you have one bad day, if you come down with the flu at the wrong time, if somebody trips you coming out of the blocks, you're done. That's it. And while I guess that's the beauty of sports, that anything can happen on any given day, you don't see them picking the Dream Team by bringing every NBA player together for a one-day tryout. Hell, what if Michael Jordan can't find his shot that day? What if he tweaks his back getting out of bed? Do you think for one second that Team USA is going to go to Barcelona without the best player in the world? Hell no they're not.

So why isn't it the same in track?

It's not to suggest that I'm the track equivalent of Michael Jordan, because I'm not. That would be Carl Lewis, and I'm not him, either. But I am the No. 1 decathlete in the world by a pretty wide margin. So like I said, for a few days I hold tight to the thin hope that maybe they'll do something to put me on the team. Maybe they'll institute some kind of one-time waiver or something. Call it the "Dan O'Brien rule." One night I even dream about getting a phone call from some guy telling me that they've pulled a few strings and I need to pack my bags for Barcelona. I jolt awake, and for a few fine seconds, I actually believe it's true.

I'm not the only one who can't fully accept this. A lot of people are trying to work a lot of different angles to somehow get me to Barcelona. Hell, because my dad's dad, Grandpa O'Brien, is from Ireland, there's even an inquiry put in about

Clearing Hurdles

the possibility of my going as part of the Irish team, but this idea is quickly shot down when we're told that I wouldn't be able to compete for the United States for the next two years at a minimum. I don't know who we think we're kidding, anyway, other than ourselves. I mean come on. Rule changes? Switching countries? After a few more days of indulging in this fantasy, I finally come to grips with the harsh truth. I'm not going to the Olympics with America. I'm not going with Ireland. I'm not going at all.

Well, at least not as an athlete.

Clearing Hurdles

The Pole Vault
You *Didn't* Hear About

I'm in Barcelona as an analyst with NBC. It's Day Two of the 1992 Olympic decathlon, and Dave has arrived at the pole vault in the hunt for a medal. It's his turn to jump, but he doesn't look good. He's limping heavily. A few weeks after the trials in New Orleans, he fractured the navicular bone on the top of his right foot, and though he's been able to gut it out to this point, I'm thinking this might be the end of the line. Through a crowd of people, I can see Dave kneeling in prayer.

"What do you think, Dan?" they say in my earpiece.

"I don't know. It doesn't look good."

But then, suddenly, Dave rises to his feet and walks to the end of the runway, pole in hand. He gets a look of pure determination on his face, pure will and defiance, before up and taking off down the runway. He's limping, his every step landing heavy and awkward, completely out of rhythm. But he charges forward. He sticks the pole and goes airborne, which is already farther than I thought he'd get, and manages to clear his opening height. He continues to jump again and again, battling his ass off, and when it's all said and done, I'll be damned if he doesn't end up clearing 16 feet, 8 inches to remain in the hunt for a medal. I think it's one of the gutsiest performances I've seen in a long time. And I don't even know the whole story.

See, what I don't know, what nobody will know until well after the Olympics are over, is that Dave has re-broken his foot. It happened when he was running the hurdles, just a few hours before the pole vault, an awkward step splintering that same navicular bone in a completely different direction. So now his foot was busted in two places. Doctors highly advised that he pull out of the competition. They said his foot was in such bad shape that even if he could withstand the pain, he was one wrong step from never walking right again. But the Olympic quest is strong. So rather than quit, Dave took a shot of Novocain directly into his arch, squeezed his badly swollen foot into a shoe that was a full two sizes bigger than normal, and gutted his way to the bronze medal.

Looking back, I'm sure Dave believed he had what it took to win the gold medal. But to do what he did under the circumstances that he did it? To not only nail that pole vault, but to finish up with a strong javelin and 1500 meters on a foot that was so numb that he couldn't even feel it hitting the ground? To me, that tells you more about Dave Johnson than if he'd climbed up to the top podium on two good feet. The decathlon, in the end, is about proving something to yourself, and with that being the last major competition of Dave's terrific career, what a way to remember yourself.

For me, I can't think of a better guy to be linked alongside forever.

Team O'Brien

17

Robert Zmelik of the Czech Republic ends up winning the 1992 Olympic decathlon with a score of 8,611, followed by Spain's Antonio Penalver at 8,412 and Dave at 8,309. I'd be lying if I said it doesn't irk me to watch the gold medal get handed to a guy who barely scored 8600, but in the end, this trip to Barcelona, though hard in a lot of ways, has been a true blessing in disguise. Now I've seen the Olympics. Felt the Olympics. Watching Dave get his bronze medal, knowing that he went through hell to get it, has lit my fire. And to watch Kevin Young shatter the world record in the 400m hurdles has thrown gasoline all over it.

Standing tall and lanky at a lean 6'6", Kevin's legs are spider long. I've jogged next to him before, and even then, when we're just cruising, it's impossible to keep up with him without working twice as hard. He averages almost nine feet per stride, a true bounder who requires just 12 strides between hurdles, even more efficient than the 13-step method Edwin Moses perfected. Moses is the undisputed king of the 400m hurdles, but even he never went under 47 seconds. Nobody in the history of track and field has. So to watch Kevin go out in 46.78 seconds is mind-boggling. The best 400-meter I've ever run in my life came at the world championships in Tokyo. I ran 46.53, without hurdles! This 46.78 Kevin has posted is nuts. I don't think anyone will ever touch that mark. And it's got me to thinking.

I want to break the decathlon world record.

I mean, I've always wanted to break it. But now I *really* want to break it.

It goes against the advice of Jackie and Bob Kersee, who called me after I lost in New Orleans to stress the importance of patience.

"Don't try to go out and prove something right away," they said. "Give it time. Rest."

But there's no rest for the weary, and the young athlete knows no patience. How am I supposed to come to Barcelona and watch Zmelik win with 8,611 and witness all these inspiring performances and not want to respond? I can't. I'm ready to go. I find Sloan and Keller, who've also made the trip to Spain, and ask them where the next meet is.

"Talence, France," Keller says. "The DecaStar Invitational."

It's a pretty prestigious meet, and even better, Keller thinks most of the guys who just competed in the Olympics are going to be there, including Zmelik.

"Perfect," I say. "How do we get in?"

It just so happens that the DecaStar meet promoter is here in Barcelona, and when we find him, I make no bones about what I'm coming to France to do.

"I'm coming to break the world record," I tell him. "And I'm *going* to do it."

Promoters love this kind of talk, because it gives them something to sell. And sell it he does. The minute I land in France I get taken straight to a radio station, where everyone is talking about my prediction. It's all over the French media.

The headline in the paper reads, "Mission Impossible?"

Like I said about Tokyo, this is the way it is overseas. Track and field is big. This meet in Talence is an absolute party, the event of the year, like the Fourth of July in small-town America. There's music playing in the streets. Wine and beer stands. Banners stretching across the road. Municipal Stadium is already a cozy venue, the fans right on top

Decathlon long jump world record

of the action, but today, with a festive crowd that has swelled well past capacity, the situation is even more intimate—track organizers squeezing people in tight, shoulder to shoulder and 15 deep no more than five feet off the track.

It's loud. It's lively. And I'm ready to go.

After getting out of the gate with a 10.43 in the 100m, I proceed to break the decathlon world record with a long jump of 26 feet, 6 inches. Then I throw the shot put you already know about, the biggest pound-for-pound throw in history, and suddenly I'm a snowball rolling downhill, picking up speed, picking up energy. Just like any individual race, the decathlon is all about momentum. Lose it, even for one second, one event, and like poor Teddy Lindsley forgetting it was a four-lap race, you probably won't get it back. But if you can hang onto it, ride it out, that's when you can do some things.

After my shot put, the fans are standing on their heads, half drunk and in the mood to see something special. I reward them with a big 6-foot-9 high jump before finishing the day

Clearing Hurdles

with an unspectacular 48.41 in the 400m, my conditioning having suffered from the long training break after New Orleans.

Still, I'm well ahead of pace for the record.

"How do you feel?" Keller asks me.

"Great for now," I say, knowing that I have a second day on the way.

But then, it's always right there for me. I'm always on pace. In New Orleans I was on pace to shatter the world record and didn't even end up making the team. One slip is all it takes. I know that now. When word spreads that I'm in range of the record, organizers have to negotiate even more room for the fans at the start of Day Two. My dad has flown over to be here, but I don't have time to visit, I block him out. I block everyone out. After an almost sleepless night, I go into the hurdles mindful of every last detail, and come out with a 13.98.

This is just what I needed. It's not a huge time, but anything under 14 seconds, if only psychologically, keeps the momentum going. I'm amped as I move to the discus, maybe too amped, and I end up fouling on my first two throws, which means, just like that, I'm right back where I was in New Orleans, one more foul from being done. That's how fast it happens. For a decathlete, the normal procedure when you're down to your last foul is to take a standing throw, without spinning, just to ensure at least some points. But I didn't come here just to win. I'm here for the record. I refuse to be scared.

"Cut it loose," I tell myself. "Don't hold anything back."

And I don't, I trust my technique, going for it 100%, barely missing the right net upright and end up with a personal decathlon best 160-footer. The crowd roars. They know what's happening next. They know what went down the last time I pole-vaulted. I'm nervous. I won't even try to say I'm not. I'm seeing New Orleans in my head, the sea of blue and red shirts in the crowd. I can feel my heart beating, but again, I refuse to give in. I clear my head and charge down the runway without an ounce of hesitation, a show of defiance against what I'm feeling, and it works. I boom a big vault, then another big one, ending up with a mark of 16 feet, 5 inches.

In his French accent the announcer yells, "Five mètres!" And the fans howl again.

They know I'm close.

But I have to throw a big javelin. I can't have this thing come down to the 1500-meter. I think about all my work with Sloan, my plant leg, my axis.

"Turn one over," I think.

And I do, going two meters past my previous personal best for a mark of 205 feet.

I thrust my fist high in the air, completely swept up by the wild passion of the crowd. I need a mere 4:49 in the 1500m for the record. It's more than doable, even for me, and there's no doubt the excitement of the crowd is helping me with some of the anxiety. When I step to the line, they're already going haywire, and with each lap the noise builds and builds, until I'm 100 meters out with still 20 seconds to spare. Everyone is jumping up and down as I kick to the finish, throwing my hands in the air with a time of 4:42.10.

The announcer is going crazy, though I can't understand a word he's saying because it's all in French. Eventually I hear the only thing that matters.

"Dan O'Brien! World record! 8,891!"

The place absolutely erupts. Pure pandemonium. Somewhere my old roommate, Sean O'Connor, is shocked. Keller and Sloan rush to me, and I fall heavy into their arms. I'm completely exhausted, my lungs still heaving, but I've done it. For some, this doesn't erase what happened in New Orleans—the missed Olympic opportunity is simply too big to forget. But for me, this feels even bigger than the Olympics. I have successfully gone where no man has gone before. The only person prouder than I am is my dad. We ride around the track in the back of a corvette, a victory lap for all time, and the smile on his face is priceless. It's a smile that says, "My son just broke the world record," and it makes me glow inside. I doubt I'll ever feel as close to my dad as he wants me to, or even as close as I want to, but for this day, for this moment in time, there is nobody else I would rather have sitting next to me.

World record team

I don't know why I can't find the words to tell him that.

A few weeks after I get back to Idaho I get a call from an old friend in Klamath Falls. He says the town had planned a huge celebration in anticipation of my winning the gold medal. They obviously called it off after New Orleans, but now, in honor of my breaking the world record, it's back on. They send a private jet to Moscow to pick up my coaches and me and fly us back to Klamath, where we arrive to something of a hero's welcome—the sidewalks lined with thousands of people, marching bands playing in the street, the whole scene playing out beneath a homemade banner that reads, "Congratulations Dan!"

To be honest, I'm having a hard time holding the tears off, as this has to be the nicest, most touching thing that anyone's ever done for me. To see this many people coming out to support me, to have grown men telling me they were heartbroken when I missed that pole vault, it makes me feel like maybe I'm not so alone after all, like maybe a lot more people care about me than I ever thought. I see so many familiar faces. Old teachers. Coaches. Friends. But the one face I've never seen before is that of Miss Klamath County, Leilani Sang, who is just about the most stunning girl these two eyes have ever seen. With her Hawaiian skin and a shiny tiara sitting atop her golden brown hair, she looks like an honest-to-God princess.

"Hello, Dan," she says. "Welcome home."

We have that moment where we both smile shyly, neither of us wanting to look away.

Is there something happening here?

For the rest of the week, Leilani is my official tour guide, introducing me when I make appearances and give speeches, and in all the downtime I'm learning a little bit about her. She's a lot younger than me, for starters, 20 to my 27. Her family comes from the Big Island. She grew up right here in Klamath Falls, goes to college at Oregon Tech, loves animals, wants to be a marine biologist, and . . . she's seeing somebody.

I guess I shouldn't be all that disappointed or surprised that she has a boyfriend, as a girl like Leilani doesn't stay single. And besides, I, too, have been seeing someone for a while. But right now, I can hardly remember what she looks like.

I tell Keller, "This Leilani girl is incredible."

He smiles and says, "Don't go falling in love."

Might be too late.

The coolest part of the weekend is a track clinic that we put on at Klamath Union. We work on all different events, kids running and jumping all over the place, and toward the end we do a one-mile race. We even call it the "Run for Fun." To see all the kids at the line, to see the excited looks on their faces, to hear the chatter of the parents, it takes me back to that day at Merrill High, the day it all started. One guy says he was actually at that game some 16 years ago, and he's been following my career ever since, as everyone in the town has.

"You've made Klamath proud," he tells me. "And not just for your winning. The way you handled that loss. The way you didn't make any excuses and congratulated the other guys in the interview. That was so classy."

It might be the nicest thing anyone has ever said to me.

These few days at home have been awesome. I've gotten a chance to see my family, to have us all back together like the old days, the days I miss more than I let on. Everywhere I've gone people have been encouraging me, telling me to keep fighting, making me feel like I've got an entire town in my corner as I begin this new Olympic quest. It's amazing how good it can feel to come back to a place you were always trying to leave.

But unfortunately, it's not all good news.

As I prepare to head back to Idaho, my little brother pulls me aside. He looks upset.

"What's up, man?" I ask him. "You OK?"

"No," he says. "I'm not. I'm getting a divorce."

"Oh, man. I'm sorry. That sucks."

"It really does, dude. I'm hurting pretty bad."

Tom is all heart. He wears it on his sleeve. He's emotional and loving and sensitive and just about the best family man you could ever ask for. Turns out his wife has been running around on him, which pisses me off. I hate to see Tom hurting like this. I wish I could help.

I get an idea.

"Man, why don't you come stay with me in Idaho for a while?"

"Yeah?"

"Yeah. It'll be fun. Maybe you can start over a little bit, get away from some of this."

"You wouldn't mind?"

"Of course not, man. I'd love to have you."

So he does. He stays in my spare bedroom, and though I try to give him money, Tom is a proud man. He goes right out and finds a construction job, works his tail off, and then every weekend drives some six hours to Pendleton, Oregon, to see his kids. Kyle's five, Kalie's three, and Lord how he loves those kids. When he talks to them on the phone, he smiles and cries at the same time. Whenever he can, he brings them back to Idaho with him, and when he puts them to bed, he lays there for hours just watching them sleep.

One night I say to him, "Dude, you have to get some sleep of your own."

All he can do is smile, as if to tell me that I just don't understand.

"I can't waste one single second that I have with them," he says.

Then he kisses Kyle's forehead and puts his head back down on the pillow. He's not going anywhere. Tom has to be the best father in the world. If he has, in fact, always looked up to me, then right now it's the other way around. Right now, as I watch him fighting tooth and nail for his kids, I am so proud to be his brother.

18

It never ceases to amaze me how people always have to dwell on the negative. It's like they can't help themselves. Instead of focusing on the nine events that I'm pretty good at, all people want to talk about is the 1500m, the one event I'm not very good at. Instead of focusing on the world championship that I actually won, it's all about the gold medal that I *didn't* win. This is a foreign way of thinking to me. To me, I just broke the world record. Things are good. Yet every time I do an interview, every time my name pops up on TV or in an article, still, it's always about 1992.

As one writer puts it, "the pole vault heard 'round the world is still ringing."

People just can let go of this thing. Writers continue to call me a bust. A choker. The track-and-field equivalent of Bill Buckner. And they haven't been any easier on Sloan and Keller, basically blaming them, as my coaches, for the decision to take my opening jump at almost 16 feet. I don't get upset very easily, but this pisses me off. What happened in New Orleans wasn't my coaches' fault. It was my fault. I missed the jump. But I didn't miss it because I'm a bust or because I choked. I missed it because things happen, plain and simple, and if there's a silver lining to be found in this whole mess, I do believe that it's brought the three of us closer together.

Think about it. Until New Orleans, the three of us, as a group, had never been through something that could actually be considered trying, something that tested the resolve of our relationship, of our commitment to one another. Within our first 18 months of working together we won a U.S. and world championship and broke an American record, and things are always rosy when you're on top. But when you lose, when shit goes bad in front of the whole world, when people start throwing stones, that's when a team can start to break apart. A family never stays the same after a tragedy. It either gets stronger, or it gets weaker. We've gotten stronger. I can feel it. The merit of our bond has been fortified by a common struggle, and we're in this thing together like never before. Atlanta. '96. Us against the world.

"Let's go to work," Sloan says.

So we do, because this is the only way we know how to live. Get back in the gym. Get back on the track. Get bigger. Get stronger. Get faster. I feel like I'm back in the role of the underdog, which is where I've always been most comfortable. I like being the kid from the small high school going up against the big guns from Sutherlin. I like being the guy who wasn't recruited. I like feeling like I have something to prove. It's but one more way for me to connect with Sloan, who was the ultimate underdog in his day. He was never supposed to qualify for the Olympics in '68, but at the trials, which were being held in Lake Tahoe so the athletes could acclimate themselves to the high altitude they would face in Mexico City, he ran himself delirious in the 1500-meter to barely scrape his way onto the team.

"When that thing was over," he tells me, "I honestly couldn't see straight."

And I believe it. I absolutely believe he was willing to push himself that hard. Hell, at 50 years old he's still balls to the wall in the gym and on the track. Sometimes it's all I can do to keep up with him. Our workouts are fast paced, high intensity, very little rest between lifts. And there's nothing fancy about what we do. We're down and dirty. Old-school iron. Push-ups. Sit-ups. Pull-ups until our hands are raw. One of the most grueling things we do is the VersaClimber, a machine that's basically like climbing straight up the face of a mountain. While Sloan stands off to the side jumping rope, I go as hard as I can possibly go for 30 seconds on the Climber, grinding to a point where I can hardly breathe. We take 30 seconds of rest and then switch, Sloan to the Climber while I take to jumping rope. We go back and forth like that until our legs and lungs finally give out, until our bodies simply refuse to cooperate any longer. By the time we walk out of the gym, we're so drenched in sweat that you'd think we just showered with our clothes on, and to me, there isn't a better feeling in the world. I grab an ice bath and a Bear massage, and the next morning I'm back at it on the track with Keller.

Sprint intervals. Plyometrics. Hurdles. Long jump.

My schedule is unrelenting and bloody consistent— mornings with Keller, afternoons with Sloan and Mick at Washington State, where I'm beginning to spend more and more time. Sloan's listed me as a volunteer assistant coach with the track team, so now I travel with the team and I'm a mainstay around the athletic buildings and in the weight room. I'm always popping my head into offices, chatting it up, getting to know the coaches and secretaries. Before long I've become so engrained in the campus community that the school, as part of its "Adopt a Cougar" program, has officially adopted me, making the announcement at halftime of a football game. Once again, a family has welcomed me in from the outside and made me feel like one of its own.

"You're one of us now," Sloan says. "You're a Coug."

It's everything I've ever wanted, I feel like I'm part of something, part of a town, of three towns, Moscow, Pullman and Klamath Falls all proud to call me one of their own. This, more than anything, is the exact reason I never even considered going to L.A. to train with Jenner, the reason I could never see myself living or training anywhere else. There's a sense of belonging up here. People stop me in the market just to shake my hand and chat. They honk and wave when they see me jogging. I've felt like a part of Keller's family for a long time, and I'm starting to feel the same about Sloan and his family. I eat dinner at their houses. Hang out with their kids. Sloan has season tickets to the football games, and on the Saturdays the Cougars play at home, we're there, bundled up in zero-degree weather, high-fiving and screaming until our throats are raw.

Sloan and I are really starting to click now. He's a hard ass who expects nothing less than your best, but when you give it to him, he's the easiest guy in the world to get along with. Nothing but a big kid, really. On sunny days he'll take his shirt off and hike up his shorts like the biggest nerd on earth. On the road he'll show up at the hotel swimming pool in a pair of leopard-print Speedos just to make everyone laugh. And for me, that sort of loose, laid-back release is exactly what I need, because the daily grind of what we do is so very intense. We work so hard, and the stakes are so high.

Every day Sloan asks me, "Are you the greatest athlete in the world?

There was a time when I would've told him yes, absolutely, I'm the greatest athlete in the world. But times have changed. I've been humbled. The reality of 1992 has pierced my shield of invincibility, and anytime that happens, anytime you have to re-prove things to yourself, it's a process. Sloan drums that into me every day. This is a process. Trust the process. And for me, there's something fascinating about that, something wildly romantic about the pursuit of something so grand and worthy. When I watch movies like *Rocky*, it isn't the last fight that captures my imagination. It's the training scene that comes before. The underdog shadow boxing in an empty gym. The warrior steeling himself for battle. I find more inspiration in the struggle and sacrifice than I do the actual victory.

To that point, Sloan and I decide we're going to run every stair in the Kibbie Dome at Idaho on Christmas Eve. All told that's just south of 3,000 steps, up and down 24 rows with a 200-meter run along the upper concourse between each set. It's a completely brutal workout. The concourse runs alone equate to more than three miles, and by the 12th row of stairs my legs are on fire. By the 16th row they're honestly shaking. But we refuse to stop, not even for one second, and in the end, after grinding through the last few rows on sheer will, we have managed to touch every single stair in a little less than 56 minutes. Neither of us can breathe, but as we stand hunched over, our hands on our knees with a puddle of sweat forming at out feet, Sloan manages to crack a smile.

"I'll guarantee you this," he says. "Nobody else is doing this right now."

In January I go to Ontario, Canada, and win an indoor triathlon, which consists of the shot put, long jump and 300 meters. In February I go to New York and Boston and win the

Visa-sponsored pentathlon at the Millrose Games and Boston indoor. Two weeks later, I go to the Sunkist Invitational in Los Angeles and win a mini-decathlon—50m, 50m hurdles and long jump. In March I go to the Indoor World Championships at the Skydome in Toronto and break the heptathlon world record with a score of 6,476. My best indoor season by a long shot. I continue to improve as I move to the outdoor season. Just before the '93 U.S. Championships, I run in the Bruce Jenner Classic in San Jose, where I beat 1988 Olympic champion Roger Kingdom in the high hurdles by running 13.44, which will be my fastest hurdle race ever.

Later that night, I'm out in San Jose with a lot of the other athletes. We're having a few beers and joking around, when all of a sudden we see a big group gathered around Ricky Watters, the 49ers running back. From afar it looks like he's chumming it up, the center of attention, but when I get over there I realize that the situation isn't so chummy. Rather, Ricky is up on a soapbox telling everyone how track, basically, is a joke, and that if he felt like it he could go to the Olympics tomorrow.

What an idiot.

If Ricky could, in fact, go to the Olympics, which I seriously doubt, then it would be because he's a world-class athlete, not because track is a joke. I'm always amazed by the blatant disrespect these nonmainstream sports get, like soccer in America or gymnastics. Have you ever tried a bicycle kick? Ever gone through a routine on the uneven bars? You think you're strong? You think you're fast? Try lining up next to Carl Lewis or Michael Johnson. Try long jumping against Mike Powell. Try running the sticks alongside Edwin Moses or Kevin Young, whose strides would swallow you up like a tsunami.

Then come talk to me about going to the Olympics.

The 1993 U.S. Championships are being held in Eugene, Oregon. My family is here, and I've been dealing with a stress fracture in my pelvic bone for close to three months, ever since the world indoors in Toronto. For a long time doctors couldn't diagnose the problem, which is to say they couldn't find anything wrong with me, so it was difficult to explain to my coaches why I was sitting out of practice. Nobody can ever understand how much your body hurts except you, and this thing hurts like a bitch. As it gets closer to go time, I decide I can't take the pain. I'm going to pull out.

"No," Bear implores. "Come on. You'll be fine."

"I'm telling you, dude. I can't go."

"Yeah, you can. Come on. Let me get my hands on you."

I hop on the training table and let Bear do his work. He's trying to calm my nerves as much as he's trying to work out any physical issue, reminding me that I'm the best, that I feel great, that my body's perfect, all systems go—but no, it just doesn't feel right. I think I'm done.

"You're done?" Sloan says incredulously. "What the hell does that mean?"

"It means I'm done. I can't go."

"Are you kidding me? You're just going to quit?"

"Hey, you don't have to jump with this thing. It fuckin' hurts, man."

"I know it hurts. But fight through it, dammit!"

"I'm sorry. I'm out."

"You realize this is the qualifier for the world championships, right? If you sit this one out, there goes your shot of defending your title."

"I know. I'm sorry."

The look on his face is one of complete disbelief. This isn't the way Sloan rolls. This is the guy who ran himself damn near dead to make his Olympic team. He comes from the school of the football player sucking it up and playing on a broken leg—but the major difference between the football player and me is that the football player, presumably, loves to play football. I don't love the decathlon that way. Not yet. Which obviously begs the question: is this really just a pelvic issue?

Deep down, for as much as this stress fracture is honestly killing me, I have to wonder if this is just the excuse I need to not have to deal with the pressure and stress of this day. In addition to all of my normal pre-decathlon anxiety, this is my first U.S. Championship since 1992. For the last two days, reporters have surrounded me wherever I've gone. They want to know if I'm going to be thinking about New Orleans when it comes time to pole-vault, which is the dumbest question I've ever heard in my life. Of course I'm going to be thinking about it. I'm probably going to think about that mess every time I pick up a pole for the rest of my life.

I know that if I pull out of this thing, that's what they'll say, "O'Brien couldn't handle the pressure, *again*." But right now, I don't give a shit. I'm in pain, and that's all there is to it. I find my family and let them know I'm done. Sorry you made the trip for nothing, but I'm out of this one.

"OK," my mom says. "We understand."

But not everyone else feels the same.

"Give it a go," my Uncle Jim says. "You'll be surprised what you can do."

Uncle Jim, my mom's sister's husband, has recently had a stroke, which has left him in a wheelchair. It's hard to see him so weak. I remember him as the toughest, strongest guy I ever knew. When I was a kid, he would tell me stories about being on the Navy's underwater demolition squad. He could do a hundred straight push-ups at age 60.

I think about the fight in my Uncle Jim, the fight in Tom, and I can't quit.

I go back to Sloan. "Let's run the 100-meter and see what happens."

"OK. Now you're talking."

I run 10.72 to start—not very good, but the pain is tolerable. I take one long jump at 7 meters 54, over 25 feet, and decide to play it safe and forgo my final two attempts. I'm just OK, or even a little below average for the rest of the meet, but in the end, the other guys just aren't ready to win at this level. Steve Fritz finishes second, while Brian Brophy, an NCAA champ, goes third. I win my second U.S. title with a score of 8,331, my lowest total as a professional, and even though I feel embarrassed that I almost pulled out, I'm proud of the way I fought. I've never had to compete in that much pain.

A few weeks later I get a call from my mom.

"Do I have your permission to look for your biological parents?" she asks.

"How are you going to do that?"

"The state of Oregon has a new database where you can put in your birth information, and parents can put theirs in, too. If there's a match you can contact them."

Growing up, I've never spent a lot of time thinking about the parents I'd never met. I was happy with the family I had. Thankful. And even more than that, why risk stirring up emotions you never even knew you had? Why even go there? Back then, and still today, I believe that some things are better left unknown.

And yet, when something like this is brought to my attention, when for the first time it becomes an actual real possibility that I might be able to meet the people who brought me into the world, I can't help but be a little curious. I know that Tom, in his efforts to piece his past together, has found out that his birth parents no longer live in the country, and on top of that, he also made the discover that he's actually Spanish, not Mexican, as he and everyone else had always thought. I think not knowing what you're going to find out is one of the fears, but the more I think about it, the more I think it would be kind of cool to meet my birth parents. See what they look like. Maybe ask them a few questions.

"What the hell," I tell my mom. "Let's give it a shot. What do we have to lose?"

I'm in Stuttgart, Germany, for the 1993 World Championships. My pelvic situation has given way to a right hamstring that's on the verge of blowing. This is what the decathlon does to you. It beats you to shit. But getting through the U.S. meet was a big step for me in that it gave me the confidence that I could compete and win at not just less than

100 percent, but at *far* less than 100 percent. As the defending world champ and one of the main headliners here in Germany, I'm not even considering pulling out this time.

The other big name on the men's side is Michael Johnson. A big, upright sprinter in the mold of Jesse Owens, Michael is probably as powerful a runner as I've ever seen—his mechanics almost robotically perfect, his core so strong and still that if you were to place a medallion around his neck while he was running an all-out 200-meter, it would hardly move. At the 1991 World Championships in Tokyo, I watched Michael obliterate the field in the 200-meter, running 20.01 to torch Namibia's Frank Fredericks by an incredible .33 seconds, the widest margin of victory since Jesse Owens in 1936.

It was one of those rare, truly jaw-dropping performances, and I knew right then and there that Michael was destined to change sprinting forever. That he would win Olympic gold in Barcelona seemed a complete lock, but right before his 200-meter competition he came down with food poisoning, lost a bunch of weight, and failed to even make it out of the semifinals. He was able to win a gold as the third leg on the 4x4 relay team that broke the world record, but the 200-meter was his race. That was his life. So Michael and I have that in common: we're both on a mission to exorcise the demons of 1992.

Here, Michael has decided to run the 400m instead of the 200, as the IAAF race schedule, at present, simply does not allow a runner to do both. Over the next three years Michael will lobby hard to get this changed, to allow for more time between these two particular races to give runners a shot to double up, but for the time being, figuring he's already got a 200-meter world title in his pocket, he runs 43.65 to win the 400m handily. Then, for good measure, he shaves almost a full

Clearing Hurdles

second off that time by going 42.91 for his leg of the gold medal 4x4 relay.

To this day, that is the fastest 400-meter split ever recorded.

Meanwhile, I'm worried about a young German kid named Paul Meir. He's got great hops and good speed, and with the adrenaline of the home crowd, which has been big and rowdy like a European soccer match all week long, he might be able to do something. A few days prior to the start of the decathlon, I'm at the track watching a few events with Sloan and Keller and just being here is making me anxious. Sloan can see it. By now he gets what I'm going through in these moments, that the hours ticking down to my event feel like the gradual tightening of a blood pressure cuff, and he knows it's the sitting still that makes it worse.

"Come on," he says. "Let's get out of here. Let's go over to the practice area."

Perfect. My sanctuary. My place of worship.

When we arrive, it's calm, quiet, the dusk turning to dark at six in the evening. Just to be away from the madness of the main stadium has allowed me to exhale. We walk a few laps. Talk. Laugh. Settle down on the infield to go through some light stretching—routine for the sake of routine.

"You doing OK?" Sloan asks.

"Yeah. I'm good. I was just thinking, it feels like it's been a while since we've thrown the shot put."

"You know, now that you mention it, it has been a week or so."

In times like this, my preparation is my only peace of mind. It would really make me feel better to get a few throws in. But how? I don't exactly have a 16-pound ball of steel sitting in my back pocket. Sloan spots an old shed off the backside of the track, just like the one at Oregon State where Dick Fosbury perfected the Fosbury Flop. It looks like it's on its last leg, the wood faded and splitting, like a stiff breeze would blow it over, but you never know. Maybe something's in there.

We walk over and push open the creaky door, and there, with the fading sun peeking through a small, dirty window, is something of an athlete's treasure chest. Old dumbbells. Rusty bars. Iron plates. Everything seems scattered in the most perfectly preserved way, like the remains of a forgotten shipwreck, like some great champion in black and white just finished a workout a hundred years ago. Sloan and I begin rummaging around carefully, lightly, as though not wanting to upset the spirit of the place. I come across a jump rope. A medicine ball. And then, over in the corner, we see it: an old gunmetal-gray shot put barely sticking out of the dirt. We dig it up like a buried jewel. Blow off the dust. Look at each other.

It feels like an omen.

"Can you believe this?" I say to Sloan. "Here we are talking about how we haven't thrown the shot in a while, and this rusty old thing appears out of nowhere?"

"What do you think?" he smiles. "You want to take some throws?"

"Hell yes I do."

So we head back to the field and go to work, because when in doubt, this has always been our answer to everything. Darkness has set in now, and we're basically alone in the practice area. Just the way we like it. Champions are made when nobody's watching. We only take 10 or 15 throws, just

Clearing Hurdles

1993 World Championship podium

enough to settle my stomach. Then, before we head back over to the stadium to find Keller, we go to the shed to properly return the shot to its home, leaving it exactly as we found it, in the exact same hole in the ground, filling the dirt in around it to leave it for the next thrower, the next champion, the next dreamer who's just passing through on his way to the top of the world.

Inspired and ready, the local kid, Meir, gets off to a pretty good start, going 10.55 in the 100m, but I go 10.57 and boom a 26-foot long jump to show him I'm still the boss. But with every event my hamstring is tightening more and more, and by the time I get to the 400m, it feels like a rubber band stretched to the absolute brink of its snapping point. If it's going to go, it'll likely be in this race. Screw it, I'm going to go out as hard as I can and see what happens. If it blows up, it blows up. At least then I won't have to deal with the 1500. It's funny what a little fear will make you think about.

The gun goes off and I go out fast, hard, almost trying to blow the thing up and get it over with. But somehow it holds, and I actually run a pretty decent 47.46 to end Day One with a comfortable lead. The last thing in the world I'm thinking about is '92 and the pole vault, until, of course, I get asked about it. People just aren't going to let this go. Ever.

"So," the TV reporter says, "you have a history of cracking or giving into the pressure of the second day."

"I do?"

"That's what people say. How do you respond to that?"

I look him in the eye, saying "This is a new competition, nothing like last year." And the next day I vault 5 meters 20, over 17 feet, before going on to win my second world championship with a score of 8,717. A few days later, a New Jersey tabloid puts me on the cover surrounded by a bunch of crushed beer cans. The headline?

From Chump to Champ

Not exactly one for the scrapbook.

World champ, 1993

19

By now, as evidenced by that tabloid cover, the dirty details of my life have been laid wide open, described at length in the pages of *Sports Illustrated* and *Time Magazine*. And as hard as it is to be continually reminded of all the dumb shit you've done, it seems like a lot of people have really connected with my struggles. Every week I get letters by the box. They come from all over the country, and sometimes even the world. They come from people who've been adopted. People who've battled alcohol. And, as you're about to read, people who've screwed up things far worse than a pole vault.

Dear Dan,

I am writing you this letter from state prison, where I will be for the rest of my life. I would like to ask if you would be willing to send me 5 or 10 autographed pictures that I could then sell to try to pay for my education. I am currently enrolled in correspondence courses and my grades are good. I've read about your story and all the things you've been through and I wish you the best.

I think a lot about what I've been through in my life too. When I was a child I was sent to a school for mentally retarded kids just because I wouldn't talk to anyone due to all the family abuse I was suffering. My teacher asked me about it one day, and when I wouldn't tell what was happening the principal called my house and talked to my dad. When I got home my dad beat me real bad and slit my dog's throat and said "this is what I will do to you if you tell anyone!" For weeks I talked to my dog hoping it would bring him back to life, but it didn't.

I know as an inmate in state prison I will never be able to shed the labels on me, but I am sorry for the crimes I did. Every day I have to live with the fact that I ruined other people's lives, and I will never be able to escape the guilt from that. But I am doing what I can to mend the broken bridges I have caused other people. I am doing all I can to educate myself and get treatment. I don't want these walls to stop me from becoming the person I should have been. I have changed so much, and even though I have a long way to go, I hope to make a contribution. I find that I am a talented and creative person, so I'm not a waste or helpless. But I do need your help.

Please consider granting me my request of 5 or 10 signed pictures. The address is enclosed. It would really help. Good luck with the rest of your career. Thank you and God bless.

Sincerely,

Frank

I have no idea what this guy's crime was, though it couldn't have been good if he's going to be in prison for the rest of his life. But regardless, I can appreciate his desire to move forward. I hope he got the pictures I sent. I hope they helped in some small way. I'm finding that the closer you come to achieving the success you've always wanted for yourself, the more you want to use whatever platform you have to help others do the same.

With that in mind, I've started a foundation.

The Dan O'Brien Youth Foundation is all about kids and positive activity. I'm doing appearances and fundraisers to provide scholarship money to worthy student-athletes, but the coolest thing we're doing, in my opinion, is the Citizenship Decathlon, which has been organized in conjunction with the Klamath County School District. Points are given for 10 different areas such as community service and academic improvement. Did you take the time to read to someone younger than you? Did you run for class president and play on the basketball team? I go back to Klamath to check up on the foundation, and we give out hundreds of medals for participation. One time, we give the gold medal to a little sixth grade girl by the name of Dana Henry. As it turns out, Dana was Leilani's little pageant sister when Lei won the Miss Klamath County pageant.

Speaking of Leilani, as luck would have it, she has recently become single. As have I.

"Would you like to go to my old high school to watch a football game?" I ask.

"Sure," she smiles. "That sounds like fun."

The start of something.

When I walk into the fall Visa clinic in Tempe, Arizona, I do so with pride, with the absolute belief that I'm the greatest athlete in the world. After two world championships and a world record, I've pretty much graduated from the ranks of the understudy. Now I make appearances and give speeches alongside Milt and Jenner like I'm one of them. But Jenner, of course, is quick to point out that I am *not* one of them. I have *not* accomplished what they have. I have *not* won the gold medal.

"That's the only victory that matters," he says. "Nobody cares about world titles."

Bruce has been saying this ever since my first world title— publically downplaying, if not altogether dismissing my accomplishments whenever given the chance, and I have to wonder where it comes from. Is he trying to keep me motivated, or is he trying to keep me in his shadow? Honestly, I think it's a little of both. Bruce isn't a bad guy. He's not out to get me. When he sends me his *Sports Illustrated* cover telling me good luck, telling me to seize the moment, I believe all that comes from an honest place. But I also believe that when he goes out of his way to show me his score sheet after I break his record, that also comes from an honest place. Like I said before, the guy's as proud as they come. For the last 16 years he's been the face of the American decathlon, the guy in the center of the photo, the guy giving the speeches, and when he sees people starting to anoint me, prematurely in his eyes, I think the proud champion inside him still wants to compete.

In a way, I understand that. Even respect it.

But enough about Bruce. The guy I'm really excited to hear speak is Dr. Jim Reardon, a sports psychologist that Visa has brought in to work with us. He'll go on to work with the New York Jets and Cleveland Browns in addition to his primary focus of counseling victims of traumatic stress, and he sounds like he knows his shit. Going all the way back to that class I took at Idaho, I've always embraced the mental element of performance. I've dabbled in some visualization tactics, but I've never had anyone who could really help me dig into this stuff and understand how to use it to my fullest advantage. I ask Doc if maybe he'd like to keep talking after the clinic.

"Of course," he says. "I'd like that very much."

So we do. Over the next few months, when we see each other at different track meets, we try to find someplace quiet to have a little session. We build on a foundation of deep, rhythmic breathing exercises, inhaling slowly, deeply, exhaling negative energy, my eyes closed as I run through a mental highlight reel of all my best performances. My shot put in France. My hurdles in San Jose. My 400m in Tokyo. I relive every last detail of these moments as I'm lying in bed, when I'm in the shower, when I'm stopped at a red light or in line at the grocery store. One afternoon, as I'm driving the Moscow-Pullman highway to practice, I get so lost in the thought of my 100-meter at Randall's Island, so focused on my breathing, so locked in on the sound of the gun and the feeling of bounding to victory, that I end up jolting awake just as I'm about to swerve off the road.

Perhaps behind the wheel isn't the best place to meditate.

But that's the thing: I can't help it. I couldn't stop thinking about this stuff if I tried. I guess I could save the deep-breathing routine for somewhere other than the road, but this Olympic quest? This vision of being the greatest athlete in the world? This is my purpose in life. From the time I get out of bed in the morning, the only thing I'm thinking about is getting to the track. Getting into the gym. Getting bigger. Getting stronger. Getting faster. For as Sloan likes to say: the only way to stay number one is to work like you're number two.

For me, if ever there were a time when I could potentially stray from this philosophy, when I could start basking in the spoils of success and end up losing my edge, this would be it. After all, by this point I'm making more money than I ever could've imagined. I've moved up to a large sports agency. I've scored the big Nike deal. I drive a Mercedes. I'm about to start construction on a three-level house with a Jacuzzi. But remember, I didn't tell Milt Campbell that I wanted money. I didn't tell him that I wanted to be in commercials or on the cover of magazines. I listed two very specific goals that day. I still have the piece of paper to prove it.

I said I was going to win the Olympic gold medal and score 9,000 points.

Neither of which has happened.

So the quest continues, every day, my focus sharp and narrow and completely single-minded. I've always been dedicated to my training, but now it's the whole package. It's my work with Dr. Reardon. My sleep schedule. Hunkered down in the deep seclusion of the Palouse region, at the expense of just about every other thing and person in my life, I've become obsessively committed to my routine. I've lost touch with friends. I hardly talk to my family. I spend holidays in the gym. Leilani is starting to visit me almost every weekend, and I see Tom now and again (he's doing better with a place of his own and a real nice girlfriend that he'll go on to marry), but other than that, I've pretty much closed myself off from the world.

And I find a romantic strength in that. I'm up here in the Palouse, in the snow, running up hills wearing gloves and a beanie with nothing but a core support group as companions. Mick. Sloan. Keller. Bear. Reardon. The media calls us Team O'Brien, and that's exactly what we are. A team. A family. And right now, we're bloody dangerous.

With a burning focus and a body that's fully healed, 1994 is primed to be a huge year for me. With the U.S. Championships in June, the Goodwill Games at the end of July and a return to the DecaStar Invitational to round out the summer, I've got three major meets on the schedule. Three chances to score 9,000 and break the world record. And everything I do is in preparation to take advantage of those opportunities. I go to the Modesto Relays and run second in the open hurdles. I go to the Penn Relays and throw almost 170 feet in the discus. But the thing I'm working on most is my high jump.

Sloan says I need to get better at running the turn, which is to say I need to maintain my speed as I angle in toward the bar. It sounds easier than it is. Imagine a circle about the size of the logo at the center of a basketball court, and how difficult it would be to run inside that circle, going round and round without slowing down and without drifting from the center. The only way you can do it is to lean sharply to the middle, keeping your feet outside your body, almost like those motorcycle riders who angle down to one knee in the turn. I work on it religiously.

At this point I'm more talented than any decathlete in the world. This is indisputable. But it's this attention to detail, this tireless commitment to the nuances of my craft, that is setting me worlds apart. I've grown so much over these past few years.

I've gone from a raw athlete to a technical tactician, from a desperate kid on the verge of drowning to a strong, inspired man who has finally taken control of his life. I've never been in a better place. Not physically. Mentally. Emotionally. Right now, perhaps in a way I've never before known, I am absolutely sure of my place in the world. This is exactly what I was put here for. This is exactly what I'm supposed to be doing. I feel there is nothing that can break my concentration, nothing that can even briefly splice my laser focus.

And then one day, I get an envelope in the mail. It's stamped with an Ohio postmark. The message is simple.

```
Dear Dan,

I've put some of the information together, and
think I might know who your father is. I think
he's my brother.
```

20

I can't stop staring at this letter, reading the words over and over. I don't know how to respond, or if I even should respond. A hundred things are running through my head. I wonder if this is somehow a result of my mom's little database search, which as far as I know came up empty. I look again at the postmark. Ohio. Is that where my dad lives? The guy who sent the letter has included his number, and for a second I consider picking up the phone. But what would I say? What questions would I ask? And would I want to hear the answers?

A few days later, I bring all this up to Dr. Reardon.

I tell him, "You're never going to guess the letter that I got in the mail."

As I've gotten more and more comfortable with Dr. Reardon, our talks have become as much about my personal stuff as they have about track—though he says, if we're not careful, one can end up affecting the other. He draws a big circle with a bunch of little circles surrounding it. The big circle is my track career, my world, while the little circles are all the potential distractions that are orbiting around it. Some of these little circles include my long list of endorsement obligations, my occasional partying, the fact that everybody thinks I'm rich now and is always asking me for money—and even more, the fact that I can't say no. The whole idea is to keep the little circles from leaking into the big circle, and the way we do that is by talking about stuff here, in the office, on the phone, so that when I go to the track my head is clear.

Jim Reardon and Dan

"Are you thinking about pursuing the letter?" Doc asks me.

"I don't know. What do you think?"

"It doesn't matter what I think."

"Honestly, I just don't feel like dealing with this right now. I'm in a good place. I'm dialed in at the track. I don't need this hanging over me."

"OK. I get that. So what then?"

"I'm going to send it to my mom. If she wants to check into it, fine. If not, that's fine, too. She's always been more interested in finding my parents than I have, anyway."

So that's what I do. I slip the letter back into the envelope and send it off to my mom. She wants to talk about it, of course, but not talking about it is the whole point in sending it to her.

"I'm sorry," I tell her. "I just don't have time for this right now."

"Well, do you think I should call this guy?"

"I don't know. It's up to you. But I have to get going. I'll talk to you later. I love you."

And with that, I hang up the phone and head to the track. Sloan says the greatest asset a decathlete can have is the ability to forget, the ability to put things out of your mind and move forward, and the track is where I go to do that. I remember the day my mom was driving me back to Idaho, the day she told me how she'd spotted a man in the stands who looked a lot like me, and I remember how I went back to school that very day and headed straight for the track, how I started throwing discus with Tim Taylor, how I got into the weight room and turned up the heavy metal music and started lifting with the gorillas.

Mick is probably the only athlete I've ever known who shares my passion for training. Like me, he was born with the extreme gene, the all-or-nothing mindset that can serve as both our greatest strength and greatest weakness. Incapable of doing anything half-ass, Mick will drink himself into an absolute stupor by night, sleep it off, and be running 21-second 200s the next morning—though his capacity for training has never equated to the type of success it has for me. At most major championships, he struggles to even make the semifinal round, and as long as I've known him, he's never made it to a final. But for what he's working with, for what he's been given—or *not* given—in the way of natural physicality and talent, he probably gets more out of himself than just about any athlete I've ever known.

And that's why he's the perfect training partner for me, or for anyone, for that matter. He pushes me. Inspires me. And I do the same for him. Anyone who works out with any sort of intensity, with any real desire to make real gains, knows there's a level you can go to with the right training partner that you simply can't go to alone. And that's where Mick and I challenge each other to go: to the next level, to the other side of the wall. We live by the motto that a man can always do one more of anything. One more set of stairs. One more rep on the bench. One more sprint. It might hurt like hell, but it's not going to kill you.

Or is it?

One afternoon we're doing 200-meter repeats with about five minutes rest in between when Mick decides he's going to run all six runs in 21 seconds flat or better—which, for a guy of his size and stride length, should be almost impossible.

"Mick, you're not going to run under 21," I say.

And that's all it takes.

"Fuck you, O'Brien," he says. "I'm gonna do it."

When Mick runs, there's something that glows, something you can feel, even see. It's like something inside him is burning, on fire, his face clenched, his legs whipping, his feet desperately popping against the track. He runs 21 seconds. He runs 21.3. He runs over and over again, completely hell-bent on going 21 flat or better, and finally he pushes too far. On his last pass, just as he's crossing the line in a time nowhere near 20 seconds, he literally collapses to the track like he's been shot and starts full-on convulsing. I run to him.

"Mick!" I yell frantically. "Mick!"

When I get to him he's shaking violently, his teeth chattering like he just fell through a hole in the ice. I wave the trainers over.

"Mick," I say, putting my hand on his shoulder to steady him. "Come on, man. Take a breath."

He's barely responding, and I swear to God I don't know if it's because he's scared or because he's pissed that he didn't make the time. I wouldn't wonder that with anyone else, but with Mick you never know. Personally, I'm scared as hell. To see this has shaken me up pretty good. By now Mick's sitting up, and the trainers are giving him fluids, and a few hours from now we'll be in the hot tub having a couple beers to relax.

Mick and Dan

But I suspect the vision of him crumbling to the track will remain in my head for a long time. It scares me to death that Mick is willing to push himself that far.

It might scare me worse that I'm not.

At the 1994 U.S. Championships in Knoxville, Tennessee, I score 4,738 for the second-highest first-day total ever, just nine points behind the 4,747 I scored in 1991 at Randall's Island. My 10.31 100-meter is also the best I've run since New York, and my work with Sloan has translated into a monster high jump of 7 feet, 1 inch. Heading into Day Two I'm 18 points ahead of my own world-record pace, and then, out of nowhere, the sky flies open and a flood of rain comes crashing down to the tune of a true Southern storm.

It's not an excuse. The conditions are the same for everyone. I run 13.98 in the hurdles but fall off sharply in the discus, throwing just 151 feet to lose my momentum—and in the

Clearing Hurdles

decathlon, when you're in pursuit of the highest score ever, that's all it takes. One slipup. Like trying to shoot 59 in golf with a triple bogey. I finish with a score of 8707 to win my third U.S. title. The next morning, Craig Sager from TNT asks me if I'd like to meet Michael Jordan.

Is that a question?

At the moment, Michael is playing minor league baseball for the Birmingham Barons, and it just so happens that they're in Tennessee for a series. The next morning Craig takes me over to the stadium. Michael's sitting at his locker as relaxed as a guy could be.

"Michael, I'd like you to meet Dan O'Brien," Craig says.

Michael looks at me like he might possibly know my face or name, but he can't quite place it. Maybe the commercials are ringing a bell.

"Dan just won the U.S. Championship in the decathlon," Craig adds.

"Oh, nice," Michael says, reaching out to shake my hand. "Congratulations."

"Thanks, man," I say nervously, shaking his giant hand. "It's an honor to meet you."

And it is, indeed, an honor. Michael Jordan is one of the few living legends, though he sure does look strange in a baseball uniform. In a basketball uniform, he looks flawless, even God-like. But with his tight baseball pants pulled up high and a loose-fitting jersey, he looks awkwardly tall and skinny. Almost gangly. I talk to him for maybe 10 minutes, and he's super cool. Really laid back. Says to me, "Man, that decathlon stuff looks pretty hard."

I can't help but wonder how Michael would fare on the track.

I always wonder this when I meet athletes from other sports, but with Michael, it's an even more intriguing thought given that most people, including myself, consider him to be perhaps *the* standard of athletic greatness. My guess is if you polled a thousand people asking them who the greatest athlete in the world was, at least half would say Jordan, and the other half would have him right at the front of the conversation. But honestly, is that where he belongs? At the top of the "greatest athlete in the world" conversation? I have to wonder: Is he a great athlete, or is he a great basketball player?

It's a fine line, perhaps, but in finally seeing him up close, I can't help but think about the infield at a world-class track meet. People would be amazed at the eye-popping athletes that are walking around, guys you've never even heard of, guys who are so shredded up with fast-twitch fibers that you'd think they were made of elastic, guys who can run and jump with the power of wild horses. Every year Foot Locker puts on a dunk contest for its nonbasketball athletes, and you wouldn't believe some of the shit these track guys are doing. Mike Conley? Mike Powell? You'd like to think these guys have springs in their calves.

It's no disrespect to Jordan, who's clearly a phenomenal athlete and from what I can tell a pretty nice guy, but meeting him today has only further cemented my strong belief that track athletes are the purest, most impressive athletes the world has to offer.

Though I'm sure Ricky Watters would have a good laugh at that.

I'm in St. Petersburg, Russia, for the 1994 Goodwill Games. There are big tanks sitting in the road and soldiers walking around with rifles and AK-47s. Running directly through the center of town is a giant canal with a drawbridge, and on my first day I see a nuclear submarine surface. It's massive. Easily the length of three football fields. All the soldiers moving on deck are in their dress whites.

If I thought Tokyo was a different place, Russia is another planet.

Even the language feels cold. In Spain or France, even when I don't understand what people are saying, it still feels warm and friendly. But in Russia, everyone feels like a spy for the KGB. And this is to say nothing of the poverty. With the fall of communism, the people are out of work and out of money. Our five-star hotel is surrounded by third-world famine—buildings crumbling to waste, homeless people begging, garbage-can bonfires burning in the alley. Everyone warns you not to go out at night, at least not without a big group, so when I'm not working out at the track, I spend all my time on the phone with Leilani, telling her how much I miss her and how I can't wait to get home and see her. We don't say "I love you" yet, but I think we're thinking it. At least I am.

The dire economic situation is even more evident at the meet, where there can't be more than a few hundred people in the stands. When I ask one of the English-speaking security guards what the deal is, he says nobody can afford a ticket. It's hard to get up to compete in a place as dead and empty as this, as insensitive as that sounds, but I manage to get out to another big lead, running 10.49 in the 100m and long jumping almost 26 feet. When it comes time for the high jump, Dwight Stones, who won a bronze at both the 1972 and 1976 Olympics in the high jump and is now a TV analyst, is down on the track, and we are talking about the surface and how no one in the open section of this event jumped very well, and he doesn't think I'm going to jump very high today.

"Nobody's going high on this surface," he says.

"Oh?"

He shakes his head. "I wouldn't expect much."

So what do I do? I go a personal best 2 meters 20—over 7 feet, 2 inches—en route to winning with a score of 8,715. I get my medal and go straight to the airport. I can't wait to get the hell out of Russia.

The Decathletes: Dan O'Brien, Bruce Jenner ('76), Bob Mathias ('48, '52), Milt Campbell ('56), Bill Toomey ('68) and Frank Zarnowski

21

I close out the summer by returning to France for the DecaStar Invitational, which I win going away with a score of 8,710, making me the first decathlete in history to go over 8,700 points three times in the same year. But I'm starting to become a victim of my own success. Right now I am so much better than anyone in the world—so much better, really, than anyone in history—that merely winning U.S. and world titles are expected. My only real competition is myself. If I don't break my own world record, even in my own head a little bit, it feels like a disappointment.

A disappointment that always comes back to the 1500m.

The fact is, if I could run an even halfway decent 1500, if I could go somewhere in the mid to low 4:30s, I would break the world record virtually every time I step on the track. Sloan tends to understand that it's not that easy, because he's been there, but Keller has a hard time accepting that I just can't suck it up and push. To him, it's bordering on ridiculous to watch an athlete of my caliber run 5:16.42 in Tennessee, 5:10.94 in Russia, 4:56.58 in France.

"No guts," he tells me, and the media. "That's all that is. You just don't want it."

Whether he's trying to motivate me or not, I resent that he says this. I know I could run faster than 5:07 or even 4:45, but I need to be in some real specific shape to attack 4:30 and faster. And this is what it takes to get these world records every time out. When I'm finished with a 1500m, I can hardly breathe.

But then, this is the biggest misconception about distance running to begin with—that it's all about guts, that a guy can always go faster if he really, really wants to. You might be able to shave a few seconds on sheer will, but to think you're going to shave 25 or 30 seconds in a 1500-meter just because you feel like it, to think you can just ignore your body's limitations speaks to the height of both arrogance and ignorance. Herculean efforts are for the movies. In real life, the simple truth is that when the rubber meets the road, you're going to run what your body is prepared to run. You're going to run to the shape you're in. And pretty simply, I'm just not in shape for the 1500-meter.

It speaks to the perpetual decathlon dilemma: there are 10 events and only so many hours in the day. Every hour you spend training for one event comes at the expense of another, and figuring out how you're going to prioritize your schedule, how you're going to negotiate that delicate balance of cost and gain, is the key to the whole mystery. I go hard on my field events with Sloan, which is why I vault 17 feet, which is why I'm a huge shot-putter for my size, which is why I'm one of the better discus throwers in decathlon history. I cover all my sprinting bases with Mick, our 400m work putting me in lights-out shape for anything at or less than those distances. But again, something has to give. For me, it's the 1500. I don't put in enough miles. I'm not prepared for distance. Do I want to run faster? Of course I do. But the world doesn't give two shits about how bad you want something.

If it did, then Mick would never lose a race.

Speaking of running your ass off, I'm at the high school cross-country national championships at beautiful Balboa Park in San Diego. Foot Locker, one of my sponsors, is putting on the event, and Julia Stamps—the defending champ and an absolute stud who will later go on to run for Stanford—is closing in on the victory. She's 50 meters out, struggling mightily, but almost home. And then, in an instant, she buckles, literally collapsing in a heap of pure exhaustion. She tries to get up, but she can't. Her legs are jelly, her mind frazzled. She's wobbling around like a boxer who's just had his bell rung, like Sloan in Tahoe, having run herself into oblivion. I can see in her eyes how hard she's fighting, but the body always wins. She falls back to the ground and people run to her aid as the field passes her by. She was 50 meters from a national championship.

Later that night, at the awards banquet, her mom asks me to speak to her.

"You know what it's like to lose in such a heartbreaking way," she says. "Would you mind talking to Julia?"

I get requests like this all the time, because for all my wins, I've become much more known for my one loss. I get asked to speak at luncheons and to big groups of kids and to business people, and always, always, the topic is losing. Overcoming. Getting back on the horse after you've been bucked off. And every time, I offer pretty much the same advice that I'm now giving to Julia, who is completely distraught.

"You have a lot of good days ahead of you. You just have to forget this and move on."

It's simple, even a little cliché, but it's true. You can't change the past. All you can do is think positive and move forward with the humility and hunger to do better. I like to think I've done that in my life. For all the nagging I get about 1992, I like to think I've handled it pretty well. I like to think I've forgotten about it.

Clearing Hurdles

But have I? Really?

I have to admit, to watch Julia go down, to watch her go from the cusp of her finest hour to the lowest point of her sports life in a matter of mere instants, has triggered an eerily similar flashback. I see myself in New Orleans, suspended in the air, about to crash into the bar. I am reminded of everything I lost, which, in turn, dramatizes the importance everything I'm trying to win back. In 1956, just before he left for the Melbourne Games, Milt Campbell told his mom that he would either come home with a gold medal around his neck, or he would come home in a box. In other words, he was willing to die for his dream.

I know that what we do isn't life and death, and yet, every once in a while, it can start to feel that way. The pressure of still having to hear about 1992 almost everywhere I go. The expectations I put on myself. The grind of the training. The long days. The isolation. It weighs on you without you even realizing it, and one night I need to blow off some steam. So what do I do? I head down to the bars and proceed to get completely tanked. Needless to say, it's a bad decision.

My drinking isn't near the issue that it used to be, but it's still there. It's still a little circle. I've talked about it a lot with Dr. Reardon, admitting to him the guilt I feel every time I slip up. I tell him about this vision I have, this vision of the perfect, clean, almost monk-like life that a true champion lives, and how every time I drink—or do anything not in keeping with the good, pure life—I fall short of that vision in my head.

"I feel unworthy," I tell him.

"That's ridiculous," he says. "There's no blueprint for being a champion. There's no blueprint for anything in life. No two people do anything the same."

"Well, I've had a lot more trouble in my past than most people."

"I know you have. But listen, everyone veers off track from time to time. The key is not veering too far."

But unfortunately, tonight, I've done exactly that. I've veered way, way too far. After drinking myself crooked, I stumble out into the parking lot at two in the morning, and then, just as I arrive at my truck, I slip, slide down the tailgate, and slice my hand wide open. It's everyone's worst nightmare come to life, especially Keller's, whose reaction is a knee-jerk one that immediately takes him back to the bad times. Sloan? He wasn't around for that stuff. He never saw me when I was pissing my life away. But Keller, he was there through it all. He watched it happen. And this night, I think, has triggered a flashback.

"Now?" he says. "Really? When we've come this far? When we're this close?"

"I'm sorry. Again." I say, and we try to forget about it and move on.

The good news is this: It's not as bad as it could've been. My hand will heal. I go to the hospital and get stitched up, but I'll have to pull out of the Millrose Games in New York. The meet directors aren't happy. I was supposed to be one of the main draws, the guy on the brochures and programs. A few days from now I was supposed to fly to New York to do a press tour, hitting all the radio stations and newspapers to promote the meet. I don't like letting people down. I've done enough of that. But deep down, I'm a little relieved. I could use the downtime. I decide to hole up with Bear for a few days, just to let things die down. Bear's my guy when I need to forget

Dan and Bear

about work and just chill out in front of the TV. I don't even put my shoes on for a few days. I even get into a little reading.

I've always loved science fiction books, and over the next few weeks, as my hand continues to heal, I delve into one of the all-time classics, Frank Herbert's *Dune*, which I've probably read five times. Set more than 20,000 years into the future, *Dune* is a strange, complex tale about interstellar feuds that was actually inspired by the sand dunes off the Oregon coast. It's got enough storylines to make you dizzy, but to me, the most interesting part of the book is the story of young Paul Atreides, the heir apparent to Duke Leto, who is slated to assume control of the planet Arrakis.

If he can prove himself worthy, that is.

In a psychological test of the highest degree, Paul's hand is placed inside a box. Soon, an almost unbearable pain starts to set in. He can feel the flesh on his hand melting. And all the while, there's a needle containing a deadly poison pressed against his neck. If he gives in to his natural instincts and removes his hand from the box, he dies. If he resists the urge and leaves it in, he passes the test. I can't write like this Frank Herbert guy, but let me tell you, it's an intense scene. It makes you think about the instincts we all have to pull away from our fears, to not stand in and take the heat.

In the end, Paul is able to resist the urge and leave his hand in the box, and when he's finally allowed to remove it, he's surprised to find that there is absolutely no damage. No pain. It makes you wonder: If we don't give in to our fear, if we don't give in to our pain, does it even exist? Is it even real? Paul resists what he's feeling, he leaves his hand in the box, and it's as though nothing has happened. But if he would've given in, if he would've pulled his hand out and therefore acknowledged his pain and fear as being real, would his hand then have been on fire? Really, how powerful is the human mind? Do we truly have the ability to render things real or unreal? And what does it say that I'm pondering all this with a stitched-up hand wrapped in gauze?

I'm at the 1995 U.S. Championships in Sacramento, and after going 10.36 in the 100m and 25-8 in the long jump, I'm off to another huge start. By the end of Day One I'm ahead of world-record pace, a familiar position, and I like my chances. My hand is healed. I'm in terrific shape. But when you're going for records, the x-factor is always the conditions, and when I wake up on the morning of Day Two, the conditions, to put it lightly, have taken a hard turn for the worse. In a matter of one day it has gone from 80 degrees and beautiful to low 40s and raining sleet.

"Keep your focus," Sloan tells me. "It's the same for everyone."

"Don't worry about me," I smile. "I grew up in this shit."

I run 13.84 in the hurdles and throw a big, 168-foot discus, but by the time we get to the pole vault, the wind is howling so hard that we have to reverse the direction of the pit three different times. I've never seen anything like this. The wind is literally blowing us back in mid-air, and after I make my first two heights at 15-1 and 15-9, they deem the conditions too dangerous and shut the pole vault down, essentially ending my chances at the record. If I'm able to continue jumping, if I even get near my normal 16-10 or 17 feet, I'd be well ahead of pace, but as it is I'm stuck with 15-9 and a weather delay.

"Keep warm," Sloan says.

Is that a joke? Ice patches are forming on the track, for Christ's sake. We might have to run the 1500 in skates. We have to wait two hours to throw the javelin, and though I still manage to go over 200 feet, I'm afraid the pole vault has put me too far behind pace. As I sit on a bench bundled up in a huge jacket and pants, shivering to the tune of another two-hour weather delay, I wonder if the track gods are somehow behind this weather.

I mean think about it: I'm on world-record pace in Tennessee only to have the sky fall completely open. Then, again, I'm on world-record pace here in Sacramento before record-low temperatures and a sleet-storm show up out of nowhere and prevent me from even finishing the pole vault. Call me crazy, but it's almost as though this is the gods' answer for the fact that none of the other decathletes can present any kind of challenge to me. I look up at the scoreboard, and again, I'm all by myself at the top. Nobody's even close. And though I guess this probably eases some of the stress, I have to think I'd be an even better decathlete if I had someone other than myself to compete against.

I think back to the 1991 World Championships in Tokyo, where I watched what had to be the greatest head-to-head long jump competition in history: Mike Powell against Carl Lewis. I stood ten feet from the pit, and for the better part of two hours they went back and forth, two heavyweights slugging it out, each besting the last guy's mark, the crowd in a state of pure bedlam—until finally, on his last jump, Powell digs deeper than he's ever dug and pulls out a jump of 29 feet, 4 inches for a world record that might never be broken.

Could Mike have jumped that far without Carl being right there on his ass?

Personally, I doubt it. Mike Powell is an incredible athlete, but I think even he would tell you that it was a huge boost to have the greatest track athlete in history forcing him to go bigger in every single jump. There's a momentum that's created in a competition like that. There's a back-and-forth rhythm that you can ride. For me, I wonder what kind of score I could post if every time I looked up I had a Carl Lewis or Mike Powell breathing down my neck, if I had just one contemporary rival who could keep up with me through a full decathlon, who could force me to go a few inches farther in the long jump, a few feet farther in the discus, a few seconds faster on the 1500. But in the end, I don't have a guy like that. It's just me. I wait three hours in the freezing cold to run the 1500-meter at midnight, going 5:01.02 for a score of 8,682 to win my fourth U.S. Championship.

One shy of Bill Toomey's all-time record.

On to Goteborg, Sweden, for the 1995 World Championships. Michael Johnson and I are staying at the Intercontinental. By now we've become pretty good friends. We have the same agent. We're both Nike guys. And right now, with an obvious deference to King Carl, we're by far the biggest names in track. We're the guys getting swarmed by fans. We're the guys who have a camera on us no matter where we go. We're both the best in the world, both under the same pressure of expectation, and I think there's an unspoken bond in that.

Michael and I eat breakfast together, and to watch him, to study him, is a lesson in complete and total perfectionism. Never a hair out of place. Only the finest clothes. Regular manicures. A watch that could blind you. I believe there's a psychology to this, a common mindset among these super successful people, like Jordan refusing to be seen in anything less than Armani. People like this don't settle for less than the best of anything. They hold themselves to a higher standard. They expect more.

For Michael, it's simply not good enough to win the 200m one year, then have to wait two years until the next world championship to win the 400m. He wants to win both in the same year, something no man has ever done. For the last two years he's been trying to get the IAAF to change the meet schedule, allowing more time between events to give guys a chance to run in both, and here in Sweden, specifically for him, they have agreed to do so. They're calling it the "double."

Meanwhile, I'm trying to become the first decathlete ever to win three consecutive world championships, and my anxiety is at a breaking point. There's something about test day that looms. I'm like a law student who's on the eve of the Bar exam. I've studied. I'm prepared. I've proven to be a master in the material. But taking the test still sucks. The night before the decathlon, I'm pacing. Every time I go though this I think it's never been worse, but this time I'm sure of it. This is the worst it has ever been. I have to talk to Dr. Reardon.

"You have to do something," I tell him. "I can't take feeling this way anymore."

"Dan, a lot of athletes feel this way," he says. "But the stress is often their fuel."

"I don't care. This is miserable."

Ten minutes later I'm laid out in his room with the curtains pulled, going through the most intense session of breathing and relaxation exercises I've ever done. Doc damn near hypnotizes me, and I'll be damned if I don't feel more relaxed than I've ever felt in my life. But unfortunately, it has the reverse effect. The next morning I come out flat with no energy, my lifeless, heavy legs carrying me to a 10.57 100m that feels sluggish at best. I follow that up by long jumping less than 25 feet for the first time in I don't know how long. My body feels like I just woke up from a winter of hibernation.

Fortunately, I snap out of my funk during Day Two, riding the momentum of a 13.78 hurdles to a big, 17-foot pole vault and a personal-best 207-foot javelin to secure my third consecutive world championship. I stand on the track draped in an American flag, camera flashes popping as I hold up three fingers, one for each world title. A few days later, Mick and I watch Michael run 43.39 to win the 400m, then a few days after that he goes 19.79 in the 200 to get his double. I'm glad to have seen it, though I would've just as soon stayed at the hotel. I knew that if I came to the stadium, the media would find me, and sure enough, they have. Before long I have 20 reporters gathered around me, and they're not interested in talking about my world championship. One guy speaks for them all.

"Heading into the Olympic year, how much will you be thinking about 1992?"

They all stick their tape recorders in my face.

"It's a new year," I tell them. "I'm not focused on the past. I'm focused on right now."

I tell them this, and I believe it. But surely this isn't the whole truth. As I've admitted, a guy can't go through a loss like the one I suffered without at least some lasting effects, even a guy who's as good at blocking things out as I am. And now I have 20 tape recorders in my face. And the worst part is, I know this is only the beginning. I know that the closer we get to the trials, the worse it's going to get.

On the flight home from Sweden, I begin to steel myself for all that lies ahead, for the pressure, for the memories of 1992, for the worthy challenge of seizing the moment when my time for redemption comes. And yet, this quest has become about so much more than redemption. For me, for as proud as I am of everything I've been able to accomplish, and for as much as I'll never agree with Jenner when he says none of it matters, I know that if I were to get to the end of all this and not have a gold medal to show for it, a part of me—maybe the only part I've ever truly known—will never know the peace of feeling totally whole. Totally validated. Totally satisfied. As both an athlete and a man, this gold medal is the only thing in the world that can complete me.

And so I've arrived at my test, at my intersection of fate, at my opportunity to prove myself worthy in this battle waged mostly against myself. It takes a brave man to face his fears, and though I can't say I've ever fully done that, this time I have to. This time I will summon the courage of young Paul

Atreides, the immortal man who found the strength to leave his hand in the burning box by reciting the following words:

"I must not fear. Fear is the mind killer. Fear is the little death that brings total obliteration. I will face my fear. I will permit it to pass over me and through me. And when it has gone past, I will turn the inner eye to see its path. When the fear is gone there will be nothing. Only I will remain."

As I head into the defining year of my life, this, I resolve, will be my mantra.

Dan in a fat guy suit: Jay Leno 1996

22

I've always romanticized Bill Toomey as something of an intellectual artist. A thinker. Though the title he came to hold spoke to the contrary, Bill wasn't the greatest athlete in the world. He didn't have Milt's power or Rafer's skill. But anything he lacked in those areas he made up for with imagination and preparation. He was the first decathlete that I know of to shower and change uniforms between events so he would be fresh for the next challenge. And he had this big bag that he brought to every meet.

Bill Toomey's bag of tricks, they called it.

In it was everything from dry socks to extra spikes to a good book in case there was a long delay of some kind. Bill prided himself on being prepared for any and all scenarios that might possibly be thrown his way, and with regard to the 1992 madness I'm about to encounter, Dr. Reardon says I need to take on a similar mindset.

"You need to be ready for anything," he says. "Any question. Any situation. The last thing you want is to get caught off guard at the wrong time. Like, say, at the trials. What if you show up in Atlanta and they're running a highlight on the Jumbotron of you missing that pole vault? Is that going to screw with your head?"

"I don't know. I've never thought about it."

"Well, you need to think about it. You have to be ready for something like that. Every time you turn on the TV, you have to be ready to see that shot of you flying under the bar. It's going to be everywhere. There's no avoiding it. You have to watch that highlight so many damn times that you become numb to it. Face this thing head on."

In other words, no more running from shit.

So I begin watching videos of the '92 trials. Every day, before I go to the track, I pop in the tape. I've seen it before, but only in passing. A clip here and there. I've never actually sat down with the sole intent of watching it, absorbing it, for it's not exactly a moment I'm looking to relive. But Doc says this is what I have to do, and I trust him. Sloan and Keller agree, we need to watch this thing until we are tired of it. Sloan believes so much in this theory that we put a TV and VCR in the equipment room next to the track.

The first time I watch the video, I honestly cringe. I rewind it again and again, pausing it in midair, moving closer to the screen to figure out where, exactly, things went wrong. How the hell did I miss that bar? I watch it every day, sometimes an hour straight, and every time I take it back to the beginning and let the nightmare replay, I find myself hoping, however illogically, that a movie I've seen a hundred times before is somehow going to end differently. But it never does.

"I can't figure out what happened," I tell Sloan.

"It doesn't matter," he says. "It's over and done with. You're a different athlete now."

He's right. I am a different athlete. More specifically, I'm a far different pole-vaulter. Back then, while I'd made wild improvements in a short time, I was still raw. But now I've been jumping 17 feet for four years—not that I intend to rest on my laurels. I vault for hours on end, and Sloan is constantly reinforcing how great I look, how ready I am, eliminating all possible seeds of doubt before they find the tiniest shred of life. I continue to watch the tape. I watch it lying in bed and when I'm getting dressed and when I'm eating, and slowly but surely, it's starting to work. Just like Dr. Reardon said, I'm starting to become numb to it. I don't rewind it anymore. I just sit there and watch it, again and again, almost mindlessly, the same tired image playing to such a blur that it's actually starting to bore me. Pretty soon, I might as well be watching "Leave it to Beaver" reruns.

"So how 'bout it?" Sloan says. "Are you the greatest athlete in the world?"

"Absolutely."

I believe this not because I'm brash or conceited, and certainly not because I still carry myself with that naïve, youthful invincibility I once harbored. I believe this, simply put, because I've proven it to myself. Because I've put in the time and work. A man cannot be truly confident until he has prepared beyond his inner critic, until he can look himself in the mirror, with an honest eye, and tell himself he's done everything in his power to prepare for his opportunity. And I know I've done that. I've trained my mind and body to a level most people will never know. My bag of tricks has been packed. I'm as prepared as I can possibly be.

Yet here I am, on the morning of the 1996 Olympic Trials in Atlanta, nerves getting the best of me, sobbing like a baby in Leilani's arms.

Dr. Reardon maintains that what I experienced in '92, for the sheer fact that it was so unexpected, absolutely qualifies as a traumatic event. "And when it comes to traumatic events," he says, "anniversaries are always tough." Since arriving in Atlanta, as expected, I've been bombarded with talk of '92. Not just from reporters, but even from the other athletes and coaches, everyone wishing me good luck, telling me to forget what happened last time, nobody recognizing the contradiction of telling me to forget something in the same breath that they're talking about it. And sure enough, the second I step on the track, just like Doc warned, a big fat highlight of me missing that pole vault is running over and over on the Jumbotron.

I watch it for a brief second, and I can only chuckle.

Leave your hand in the box, Dan.

I know that getting off to a fast start will go a long way to alleviate some of this stress, and if running 10.3 in the 100m doesn't qualify as a fast start, I'm not sure what does. I get through the next three events without a hitch, throwing a solid 52-foot shot put and high jumping 6-9. As I'm laying on the massage table waiting for the 400m, Sloan spots Michael Johnson.

"Michael, Michael," he says, flagging him down. "Go over there and touch Dan, will ya? He needs that golden touch tonight."

So here comes Michael, over to the training table.

"How you feeling?" he asks me.

"Good, man. Real good. I think I'm going 46 flat."

"You look good," he says. "You're going to run fast tonight. I know it."

He says it like a prophet, laying his hands on me with an almost spiritual glow. If only Mick could be here to see this. As a fellow 400-meter guy, he's in total awe of Michael. They ran in the same quarterfinal at the 1995 World Championships. Michael coasted to a 45.15, saving his legs for money time, while Mick was eliminated with a 46.61, and in all my time knowing Mick, never had I seen him so happy to lose. It was like he got his ass kicked by Ali and never wanted the scar to heal. I always laugh when I think about that, how giddy Mick was to go to the track and watch Michael run in the finals. He's over in Australia right now, trying to make his own Olympic team. I'm pulling for him from afar, and I know he's doing the same for me.

I don't end up getting my 46 flat. Michael says I just didn't go out quite hard enough, and he's right. I hung back just that tiny split second. Still, I wound up with a fast 46.84 that has sent me into Day Two, once again, on world-record pace. But I'm not concerned with that in the slightest. I just want to get through this pole vault and make the team and get the hell out of here. I hurdle strong and throw a nice 155-foot discus, and now it's time.

"No big deal," Sloan assures me as I go into the pole vault. "We're ready."

Everyone knows I've lowered my opening height to 15-1, and I'm sure that when the bar gets there, a hundred reporters and cameramen are suddenly going to swarm the pit. As I get through warm-ups and the competition begins, I get an idea. Why not take a jump at a lower height? If everyone's expecting me to go at 15-1, if the whole stadium is going to be watching at that height, why not sneak in a jump while nobody's looking? Why not go at 14-10, clear it without the pressure of a hundred reporters snapping pictures, and suck out the drama before it has a chance to build?

"I like it," Sloan says. "Let's do it."

Clearing Hurdles

Don't get me wrong, my heart's still pounding as I stare down that runway. But when I get over on my first attempt, the sigh of relief that sweeps over my body is like nothing you could ever imagine. When the bar gets to 15 feet, sure enough, a swarm of media comes running out to the pit.

"Where's O'Brien?" I hear one of them ask an official. "When's he up?"

"O'Brien already made his opening bar."

"What? He already jumped?"

"Yep. Cleared 14-10."

The guy looks over at me, and I smile. Gotcha.

I end up taking some 15 vaults before recording a final height of 5 meters 20, over 17 feet, the same height I've cleared a handful of times and at a few different major meets. I throw a personal-best javelin of 214 feet and go on to win with a score of 8,726, securing a berth to the 1996 Olympics. Steve Fritz is also going, as is Chris Huffins, who broke a decathlon world record with his 10.22 100m. I've tied Bill Toomey's all-time record with my fifth U.S. championship, and though I'm surely excited, we haven't come this far to look up now. We're not done yet. Four years ago, we made a pact, an unbreakable commitment to a three-step process: get back to the trials, make the team, and finish the job. Those are Sloan's exact words to me.

"Let's go home and get ready to finish the job."

Back in Moscow, the excitement is everywhere. Every marquee in town, from the fast food joints to the movie theatre to the university, read things like "Good Luck Dan!" and every other kind of "Go Get 'Em" message you can think of. I get standing ovations when I walk into restaurants. People wait outside my house and honk and cheer when they pass me on the street. I'm on a billboard in the middle of Moscow.

And that's just the local stuff. In every major city in the country, Fuji Film has put up a massive billboard featuring me throwing a javelin. I told you about the *Newsweek* cover, the "Mr. Olympics" headline, and I'm also on the cover of *Time Magazine* in the background of Michael Johnson's cover. Of all the Olympians, he and I are the big stories. Michael broke the 200m world record by running 19.66 at the trials and now promises he's going to deliver a double in Atlanta, and people are saying I'm the best decathlete ever. Daley Thompson has gone so far as to say he can see me going as high as 9500 points. Frank Zarnowski believes I have revolutionized the event. Of course, Jenner isn't about to jump on my bandwagon. In an interview with *Sports Illustrated*, when he was asked to assess my chances of winning in Atlanta, he said this:

"If I were a betting man, I'd bet on Dan . . . but I wouldn't bet a lot."

Again, I'm numb to Jenner by this point, but when he says this, when he tells people he "wouldn't bet a lot on me," I think it speaks to the appeal that a lot of people find in my story. I think I'm perceived as vulnerable. I think there's an odd fascination with the fact that I'm such a dominant athlete, and yet, because of 1992, because of some of the stuff I've been through, I'm the very embodiment of an underdog. And you know how people feel about their underdogs. The letters are now pouring in by the box. It seems that in me people see their own mistakes, their own regrets and ultimately, their own longing for the simple blessing of a second chance. As one lady writes:

"If you win, we all win."

And so the buildup to Atlanta has hit full stride. I appear on Leno and Letterman. I narrow in on one last week of perfect training, no mistakes. NBC sends a film crew to Pullman to conduct an interview that will air during the games, and when they ask me about 1992, if it's the reason I seem to be training with such a purpose, I tell them that it's much bigger than that. The decathlon has inspired the romantic in me. Looking back, I can't help but think it's the reason I was put on this earth, everything having happened for a reason, the rocky path I've traveled having steeled me for the ultimate athletic struggle. I tell them about the movie *Clash of the Titans*, the story of Zeus and his son Perseus, an orphan child who has spent much of his life in seclusion. Perseus has been given these powerful gifts from the gods, gifts he has been instructed to use in the pursuit of his life's purpose.

As Zeus tells him, "Find and fulfill your destiny."

I believe that's exactly what I'm doing.

Javelin

It's late on Day Two of the 1996 Olympic decathlon, and a hundred thousand people, having just watched Michael Johnson shatter the 200m world record by running 19.32 in his famous golden spikes, have turned Centennial Stadium into a scene of pure bedlam. Never, in all my life, have I heard a crowd cheer like this, and never have I seen Michael look so excited and so exhausted at the same time. The toll of a race. Of a moment. Of a lifelong pursuit. I'm the first to greet him at the edge of the track, and as I do, as I hug and congratulate my friend, as the cameras zoom in and the flashbulbs pop, I can literally feel the weight of the Olympics shifting from his shoulders to mine.

"Now it's your turn," he whispers. "Bring it home."

He turns and raises his arms to the crowd, and they erupt. Cameramen circle around him. Tears fill his eyes. And when he falls to his knees and presses his forehead against the track, as though praying to the gods who've just blessed him, every hair on my body is standing straight up. It's almost impossible not to get swept up in this moment, but I can't. With two events left, I have to keep my head right. My eyes forward. Life is in the task at hand.

After eight events, I'm leading. Though it's tighter than I would've liked. My Day One numbers looked like this:

10.5 100m, 24-9 long jump, 51-6 shot put, 6-7 high jump, 46.82 400m. Add it up, and it was a pretty average start for me, if not a little below. I ran a fast 400m in front of 90 thousand fans but I long-jumped like shit, which was frustrating. I fouled once and got conservative from there, and it cost me.

After three slices of cold pizza for breakfast and an anxiety episode for the ages, my second day, thankfully, has been pretty good. I ran a fast 13.87 in the hurdles, threw the discus 160 feet, and pole-vaulted a decent but not great 16 feet, 4 inches. Before we came into this thing we figured my average marks would be plenty, but I'm on pace to go 8,800 and I still can't shake this Busemann kid. Just as I suspected he'd do when I first saw him on the bus, he's going at this thing without an ounce of fear, like he's got nothing to lose, and he's having the meet of his life. As I was trying to get my step right in the long jump, trying to avoid a mistake, he went screaming past me on the parallel runway, hitting the board flush and booming a giant 26-½ footer.

Then he broke the world decathlon record in the hurdles. Ran 13.47.

It didn't come completely out of nowhere, as in 1994 he ran that exact time to win the Junior World Championship in Portugal. But I never expected him to do it again. Coming into Day Two I was up on Busemann by 124 points, 4,592 to 4,468, but in this one event he has trimmed that lead almost in half. That doesn't happen often. 13.47 is a monster time. I ran my 13.87 in that same heat, from the far outside in Lane 8, and he pulled away from me. I was able to regain some of my lead with my discus and pole vault, but now he's gone and done it again, throwing the javelin a hair over 219 feet to notch yet another personal best. This guy is out of his mind right now.

If the 1500m were to start right now, I would have a 30-second cushion on Busemann, and the way I figure it, I'm going to want every last second of that. Busemann's already a better 1500 runner than I am, but now, with all this confidence and momentum he's built, who knows how low he might go. The last thing I need is for this entire quest of mine, this lifetime of work and dreams, to come down to one 1500m race against a rubber-legged kid running with his hair on fire. So my task is simple: If I don't want to give up any more points to Busemann, I have to match his javelin. I have to throw at least 219 feet.

Which, incidentally, is farther than I've ever thrown in my life.

To me, the fact that my gold medal will be decided, largely, by an event that was once one of my worst is interesting—a symbolic test of how far I've come, from athlete to decathlete. Over the years I've worked my ass off to make these last few events leading into the 1500 some of *my best, and I've done it for precisely this reason. I want to kill people, bury them, leave them without a breath of hope before I have to die myself. The stadium is still buzzing after Michael's performance, a hundred thousand people just waiting for another reason to explode. But I block it out as best I can. I go to that place in my head where it's just Sloan and me, nobody else, on the track in Washington, because the bigger the stage the more important the little things become. My first throw sticks in the ground at 212 feet.*

It's not good enough. At that mark my lead over Busemann would shrink to about 20 seconds, which is getting into the danger zone. I look around the stadium. Not an empty seat to be found. Everyone still stirring, vibrations of noise and energy rolling like waves, and I decide it's time to ride it. Time to let it in. A slow, rhythmic clap begins to spread through the crowd, moving from one section to the next, and soon the entire stadium is up and clapping to the tune of a deep, bellowing drum. As the excitement builds, and builds, and builds, I grip my javelin with a determination I've never felt, my emotions walking a fine line between composure and chaos.

"Finish," I remind myself. "Get around and finish the throw."

I take a deep breath and charge toward the line, my javelin next to my eye, I hop in to my penultimate step, planting my left foot hard and turning one over like never before, screaming violently through my release. The javelin sails through the air in slow motion, cutting clean like a knife, sticking in the ground like a dagger to the heart. I know it's good. But how good? The whole stadium is on pins and needles as we wait for the mark to appear on the scoreboard.

And then it does. 219.6 feet.

Boom! The crowd explodes like a bomb as I raise my arms and begin jumping around in celebration, my reaction fueling their reaction. I look across the track and see Keller and Sloan and Leilani. They're celebrating, jumping up and down and hugging, a moment in time I will never forget. With everything on the line, when it mattered the most, I have just thrown the finest javelin of my life. And barring something completely crazy, I have just won the gold medal.

23

So here I am, back where I started this thing some 40 hours ago—on a quiet, empty practice track in the shadow of the Olympic stadium, my nerves a total mess. It wasn't 15 minutes ago that we were throwing a party, everybody high-fiving and screaming, Mick jumping around like a wild man in the wake of my javelin. For the briefest of moments, the pressure was off and I was on top of the world. But then Keller pulled out the score sheet. Started running the 1500-meter numbers. And just like that, the air went out of the balloon. As usual, the mere mention of this race has triggered a knee-jerk, gut-level feeling of complete and total dread.

"We need 4:38 for the world record," Keller says.

I nod half-heartedly. I'm not ready to deal with this yet, but we have to.

"What's my cushion on Busemann?"

"Thirty-four seconds."

"Do we have any idea what he's going to run?"

"He ran 4:28 at the European championships."

So the math is simple: If he runs 4:28, I need to run 5:02. Give him 10 seconds for the performance of his life, and I need to go somewhere in the low 4:40s or even high 4:30s to feel really safe. We decide on 70-second laps to start, a 4:23 pace if sustained. I won't sustain it, of course, but if I can manage to stay there for a few laps and then hang on late, perhaps I can break the record.

"So it's a plan?" I say to Keller.

"It's a plan."

Good. Now we don't have to talk about this anymore. For the next 40 minutes, until it's time to start my warm-up, I don't even want to think about this race. I want to relax, or at least try. It's been a long day. A long two days. I'm completely exhausted, and yet, at the same time, completely wired on adrenaline and nerves, a combination that has me jittering like I've had about 50 cups of coffee. This is why Bill Toomey used to shower between events: to clear his head and start fresh, come out recharged, a new man for a new event. I tell Sloan I need a minute.

"Everything OK?" he asks.

"Yeah. Just let me know when it's time to get started."

"Sure thing. Take your time."

I move to the place I can always go for peace, to the track, where I begin walking laps beneath the dim glow of old, fading lights, some of which have burnt out completely. I'm trying to breathe, trying to relax, but how does one relax during a stay of execution? How do you keep from obsessing about the fate that awaits? You would think the excitement of what I'm about to accomplish, what I'm about to finish, would be enough to ease my 1500-meter anxiety—but in fact, it's making it worse, the idea that I'm actually this close to a gold medal is making my stomach fizz like a shaken soda.

I move from the track back onto the infield. D-zone. I take off my shoes and lie down on my back. I put a wadded-up T-shirt behind my head as a pillow. I close my eyes. And when I open them, Bear and Mick have joined me. Together, for the next 10 minutes, we exist in a state of almost complete silence, three friends staring off into the bright lights of Olympic Stadium, listening to the rise and fall of the distant cheers.

It should be the romantic moment I've always dreamt about. But it isn't. Because what they don't tell you about dreams is that they're only warm and cuddly when you're lying in bed. In real life, dreams are gritty. Intense. Full of pressure. As I sit here in the minutes preceding my finest hour, I'm not reflecting upon the journey. I'm not cherishing the moment. Because in the end, there's no moment to be cherished. There's only a part of me that would give anything in the world for this to be over, and another part that wishes it would never start.

And all the while, the clock ticks.

I move to the training table for one last Bear massage. As he rubs me down, I slip into brief moments of comfort, but then, in an instant, I'm startled back to reality, the cloud of my impending doom having floated back over my head. It dances above me in a taunting manner, this cloud. It laughs at me in a sick, devilish tone, playing me to a merciless tune. I said it would be different this time. I said I would summon the spirit of the great Bruce Jenner, who stared down the 1500-meter barrel with an unflinching nerve. But indeed, we all have our demons.

I jump off the table. Shake out my legs. Take a deep breath.

"Listen," Bear says. "Before you get going, there's something I want to tell you."

"What's up?"

"Well, I just want to thank you for letting me be a part of all this. To be here with you, at the Olympics, this means more to me than you'll ever know. I'll never forget it."

For me, if there is any comfort to be found, it is in these words. I've let a lot of people down in my life. But to know that

I've given at least something back to these guys who mean so much to me? To know that I've brought them along on a journey very few people ever get to experience? I can't even tell you how good that feels. It feels like one of the truly meaningful things I've done in my life.

I tell Bear, "I couldn't have done it without you, brother."

And a brother he surely is.

Our motto for the 1500 is simple: go to the line sweaty. Mick and I jog two laps, always two laps, and he can't quit jabbering about my javelin and Michael's 200-meter and how I was the first guy to greet him at the edge of the track. Mick's a fool for the excitement of all this, but I'm hardly listening to a word he's saying. When Sloan said a decathlete's greatest asset is the ability to forget, he wasn't just talking about the bad events. He was talking about the good events, too. The great ones have a way of blocking everything out except right now. Life is in the task at hand. More and more I'm sinking myself into the place I hate to go, the place where I commit to this race and everything I'll go through during it.

But as I said, Mick's another story. He simply can't contain his excitement.

"Here we go!" he screams as my warm-up concludes. "You fuckin' ready, O'Brien?"

I look at him and chuckle. One day, someone's going to tighten that screw in his head.

"Come on, man!" he yells again, pushing me in the chest to pump me up. "This is it! Are you fuckin' ready?"

"Yeah, man. I'm ready. I feel good."

"Just think," he says. "Thirty minutes from now, you'll be a legend."

The word stops me in my tracks. *Legend*. It's almost too big to say, to hear. Long have I imagined the day when my name would rest alongside the likes of Mathias and Thorpe, Rafer and Toomey, Jenner and Milt, and in this moment, in this one huge word, Mick has reminded me of how close I am to making that happen. I think about Milt and how he lost at the 1952 Olympics before winning in 1956, how Rafer lost in 1956 before winning in 1960, how Jenner lost in 1972 before winning in 1976. In the decathlon, strength is found in the struggle. Winning is found in the losing. For 1992, for the road I've traveled, I've paid my dues. Taken no shortcuts. As I make my way over to my coaches for one last meeting, I do so with the renewed perspective of a man on the cusp of something he has absolutely earned.

"OK, Danny boy," Keller says. "Here we go."

We go straight into strategy, revisiting our pace and plan to assure complete clarity on both. Seventy-second laps to start. Stay there for as long as we can, then hang the hell on. And for God's sake, keep an eye on Busemann. Don't let him get more than a 100 meters ahead. With the meet he's having, who knows what he's going to run. We come in for a team handshake, like we've done so many times, and in the weight of our stares, as we all lock eyes, you can feel the intensity. This is it. This is what it's all about. As we break our huddle, Sloan quickly pulls me off to the side. He's got something he wants to say.

"You know," he says, trying not to get choked up, "my dad never got to see me win a gold medal. I was never able to give him that. But I know he would be so proud that I'm here with you tonight."

He pulls out a pen, and in the bottom corner of my number, he writes the letters DS.

Donald Sloan.

"So if you get to feeling like you're alone out there," he continues, "all you have to do is look down. My dad will be with you every step of the way."

The scene beneath the stadium is busy, hectic, like Grand Central Station. Athletes are warming up. Doctors are giving treatment. Officials are running around on walkie-talkies. I see Dr. Reardon. I go to him, bury my head in his chest. He puts his hand on the back of my head like a child.

"Relax," he reminds me. "This is exactly where we knew we'd be. We're ready."

And then I hear it. That deep Texas drawl. My man Shirley Crowe.

"All right, boys, I know you been waitin' a long time now. Let's bring it on in."

We start the walk up the tunnel, the stadium rumbling above. It's a heavy, thunderous echo that's pounding against the walls like an Indian drum solo. I glance at Busemann, who looks pretty nervous himself, looking as if the days have weighed pretty heavily on him as well. We pause briefly at the stadium entrance. My heart is pounding. And when we step out of the tunnel, a sound that was once a heavy, muffled echo explodes like a bomb, as though I've removed my earplugs at a rock concert. The energy. The noise. It's an assault on every sense in your body—the stadium a living, breathing animal.

As we walk around the track to the start line, it's like walking up the 18th fairway at the Masters. Everybody stands and cheers as we wave and smile and tip our hats. I'm calm on the surface but kicking like hell underneath, like a duck, and Busemann's smiling in that "aah shucks" kinda way. I toss my hat into the crowd, causing a mad scramble. As I start to strip off my sweats, I spot somebody bolting past security and onto the track. I look closer.

Holy shit! It's Tom!

I jog over to the rail that sits right up against the track, and he immediately throws his arms around me and we break into prayer. It makes me think of Dave Johnson and his guys praying before the 1500 at the 1990 Goodwill Games. It certainly worked for them that night. Tom, being the more spiritual of us both, goes for one of his favorites: Philippians 4:13. *I can do all this through Him who gives me strength.*

"Please, Lord," Tom says, "give my brother wings tonight. Give him wings so he can fly around that track."

He holds my forehead firm against his, as though it's possible to pray extra hard, and as I feel his spirit passing through me like an electrical current, I'm compelled to recall the day my dad told me that if we could somehow put Tom's heart into my body, we'd have the greatest athlete in the world. Tom tells me he loves me and runs back to the stands before he gets arrested, and with that, I am left to a place I've spent so much of my life: surrounded by people, yet completely alone. As I walk to the line, there's nobody left to help me. My ultimate date with destiny has arrived. It's just me and this race. One more time. I guess it's only fitting that in order to win this gold medal, in order to conquer this game I've been playing for so long, I would have to slay the beast at the end.

"Runners, on your marks."

Bang!

1500-Meter

Almost immediately, the whole pack goes right to the rail, but I steer out into Lane 2 to get away from trouble. For a lot of guys, the 1500m is a dogfight. They want to go to the front and keep up with the pack, but for me, it's a personal fight. I just try to find my pace and wait to get tired, and that's when the grind starts. Tonight I feel pretty good through the first lap. I run 68 seconds while Busemann goes 62 or 63, though I seriously doubt he can maintain that. Or at least I hope he can't.

All is fine until about halfway through my second lap, and then it hits. That feeling I know all too well. My legs start to get heavy as it suddenly becomes harder and harder to get a full breath, and now it's a fight. I start to fade pretty quickly. That's how it happens at the end of a decathlon. Your body is already so tired that when the first wave of fresh adrenaline wears off, you fall off a cliff. I run 73 seconds on my second lap, and now I'm hardly even looking at the clock. Forget plans. Forget pace. Forget the world record. Just don't let Busemann get too far away, and get through this thing 10 meters at a time.

As I come to the 100-meter mark on my third lap, from what I can tell, I'm about 10-12 seconds behind Busemann, and now the crowd is starting to pick up. Just like runners, they long for the final lap. As I cross the line, I get a slight second wind, just for a second, because now I only have one lap to go, and anyone can do one more of anything. I'm probably 15 or 16 seconds behind Busemann now, and at 250 meters I start to push. I have almost nothing left. I'm totally exhausted. But the crowd is trying to lift me. I can here Sloan saying "finish strong, it will be what people remember."

Like my mom said, people want a reason to cheer.

Suddenly I'm Seabiscuit charging down the stretch, flashbulbs popping, a hundred thousand people screaming, an entire world glued to their TVs. I see Busemann cross in around 4:31, so unless I blow an Achilles or get picked off by a sniper, I've got this. I get to 50 meters, 40 meters, 30 meters. I swear I can hear Sloan and Keller. Finish! Finish! *I'm on pure fumes, but I'm pushing because this is the moment that will live forever. And when I finally cross in a time of 4:45.89, when the crowd erupts and I go straight to my knees in a state of complete and total exhaustion, I do not feel joy or ecstasy. I feel only relief.*

Finally, I can stop running.

I want to share the victory with the crowd that helped me stay pumped when I needed it the most, so I jog back up the straight stretch waving and holding up one finger. The whole stadium is cheering, and at once, the emotion hits me. I go to one knee, put my head in my hands, and start sobbing like a little baby. I've seen people cry after they win some kind of championship, and I always wonder if it's totally real or just a little bit for the cameras. Now I know: it's real. My mom and my brother and sisters are on the other side of the track, at the start line, because we couldn't get that many tickets in one section, but all my guys are here at the finish. Security ushers my dad onto the track. I hug him and give Leilani a kiss. And from there, one by one, I have a moment with each member of Team O'Brien.

Sloan: "Way to finish. I'm proud of you."

Bear: "I knew you could do it, brother."

Keller: "You're a true champion."

Mick: "What'd I tell you, mate? Fuckin' legend."

I move through drug testing and my interviews in a complete dream state, almost like an out-of-body experience. People are coming up to me from every direction. Michael Johnson. Steve Fritz, who has barely missed a bronze medal. And it's not too long before I remember that I didn't bring my ceremonial uniform—the uniform you wear to receive your medal—for fear of jinxing myself.

Luckily, I'm able to borrow Carl Lewis' uniform at the last minute, and the next thing I know I'm standing on the tallest podium inside Olympic Stadium as a hundred thousand people go crazy. Now, this part? This is exactly as you imagine it in your dreams. This is surreal. I bend *down as they place the gold medal around my neck, and if I tried a million times, I could never explain what this feels like. All I can say is it feels like an ending and a beginning at the same time. As my old trumpet-player head bobs to the beat of the most beautiful national anthem I've ever heard, I am certain that my life has changed forever.*

When I wake up tomorrow, I'm going to be a totally different person.

Shot put

1500-meter

Emotion

Celebration!

O'Brien & Botkin   288

Mom

Dad

Brother Tom

Clearing Hurdles

24

Almost 14 years later

It's 9:30 on a Saturday morning in the spring of 2008, and I'm completely beat. I'm dripping sweat. My legs are jelly. For the last two hours I've been climbing stairs and running 200-meter intervals on the track at Arizona State, where I'm scheduled to meet a local sportswriter, Brad Botkin, for an interview at 10:00. Before he arrives I decide to push through one more set of stairs. Halfway up the 10-story grandstands my legs are burning, begging me to stop, but I have to keep going. I'm 42 years old. I haven't competed in a decade. And still, I have to keep going.

Something isn't finished.

Maybe 10 minutes later, Brad pulls up. We introduce ourselves. Shake hands. He says it's an honor to meet me, that he was so excited when his editor gave him this assignment. He was in junior high when the Dan and Dave commercials came out. He remembers them like they were yesterday. Which is funny, I tell him, because it feels like they were yesterday, too. That we filmed those commercials nearly 20 years ago is a trip, and the fact that it's been almost 15 years since the Olympics is even crazier. I wonder where the time went. I wonder what, if anything, I did with it. And as it happens, this is what Brad has been assigned to find out: What the heck has Dan O'Brien been up to?

So I give him the basics. I'm a volunteer assistant coach for the Arizona State track team. I do some work with USA Track

& Field and the U.S. Olympic Committee. I'm a motivational speaker, a personal trainer, a television analyst, and I live in Scottsdale with Leilani, who I married in 2002.

"I'm doing a lot of stuff," I tell Brad. "But at the same time, I'm not really sure what I'm doing."

I can see this answer has Brad's wheels spinning. What I don't know yet, but what I will quickly come to learn, is that Brad's about as curious as they come. He asks a million questions, and like me, he longs for answers. This, in fact, will turn out to be one of the many things we have in common. Right away we learn that we come from the same neck of the woods, with Klamath Falls sitting just a three-hour drive from Brad's hometown of Eureka, California. Brad's dad used to fish on the river that ran behind my house. Before Idaho signed me, I nearly went to junior college in Eureka. One of Brad's old media buddies, Tag Wotherspoon, used to do the radio for my high school football games.

"But you want to know the craziest coincidence of all?" Brad says.

"What?"

"You actually met my wife before I did."

"Really? How?"

"When she was 10 her dad took her to a track meet to see you and Bruce Jenner. You signed an autograph for her. Her dad still has it framed. Small world, huh?"

It's a small world, indeed. There's an immediate comfort between Brad and me, as though we've known each other far longer than the 15 minutes we actually have. Before long we've moved from the stands down onto the track, and now we're just walking and talking. No more interview. No more tape recorder. Now we're just two guys shooting the shit, and it's the start of a good friendship.

Next thing you know, we've been circling the track for an hour and a half, and in that time I've essentially given Brad the Cliff notes of the same story you just read. I've told him about my adoption and my drinking. I've told him about the day Milt Campbell asked me what I wanted. The day Coach Keller pulled me in off his porch. I've told him about the great memories, the not-so-great memories, the mistakes I made and the lessons I learned, and how at the end of it all I stood proudly atop the Olympic podium with a gold medal around my neck and thought to myself that my life was about to change forever.

"And did it?" Brad asks.

"No," I admit. "It didn't."

Sure, I basked in the glory for a while. I did the talk-show circuit. I played in the celebrity golf tournaments. I walked the red carpet at movie premiers. But when it was all said and done, when the excitement died down and the world went back to real, I once again felt incomplete, like the void the gold medal was supposed to fill was still there. You hear stories about Bruce Jenner leaving his vaulting poles at the stadium after the '76 Olympics, because he knew he was done. He was ready for the next phase of his life. But I found out very quickly that for me, there was no next phase. I had no idea what to do with myself. And that scared me. I went scrambling back to the only life I knew the way an asthma patient goes for an inhaler.

At 30 years old, I became the oldest decathlete in history to win the Olympic gold medal, and after taking 1997 off to ride the glory train and rest my body, people said I'd been away

Clearing Hurdles

Dan and Michael Johnson at the victory party, Planet Hollywood, Atlanta, 1996

too long. At 32, I was far too old to remain the best in the world. Still, I went to New York in 1998 and broke the Goodwill Games record with a score of 8,722. On the strength of that win, I finished the year as the No. 1-ranked decathlete in the world for the sixth time, which remains a record to this day.

"And that was it," I tell Brad. "That was the last major event of my career."

"So you haven't competed in 10 years?"

"Not to speak of. No."

A few days later, Brad's article comes out. It's not what I expected. It's not just an update on what I'm doing. He writes that he's fascinated with the mindset of a man who would continue to train so maniacally 10 years removed from his last event. He writes, "What drives a man like that?" It's a complicated question. As I tell Brad when I call to thank him for the article, there's a fine line between doing something because you love it and because it fulfills you, and doing it simply because you don't know how to do anything else. And ultimately, when I go to the track for hours and hours and work myself into a lathered stupor, I'm walking that line.

I invite Brad to one of my speeches. When I glance at him in the back, I can see him listening intently. Afterward we grab a pizza. We talk about goals and dreams. And over the next six months, as we become friends, as we lift weights and play golf and go for happy-hour chicken wings at a place called Uncle Sam's, we continue to do so.

I ask Brad, "What do you want?"

"I want to be a writer," he says.

It's like déjà vu all over again. I can see myself in San Francisco telling Milt that I want to be a great athlete. I tell Brad the same thing Milt told me.

"You're already a writer. What do you really want? Specifically? Think about it for a while. It's the most important question you'll ever ask yourself."

I enjoy talking to Brad about this stuff, because I can see the ambition in him. Just the way he talks. The way he listens. The way he talks about doing "something that counts." It reminds me of the fire I felt when I was young and hungry, the fire I was so desperate to never let burn out. I continue to fill him in on my story, taking him back to 1998. After I won the Goodwill Games, I knew my body wasn't what it used to be. I knew I was breaking down. But I thought I could defy the knee surgeries and the sometimes crippling back pain and the plantar fasciitis that often made it hard to walk.

Clearing Hurdles

In 1999 Leilani and I bought a vacation home in Scottsdale, Arizona, but while she was spending most of her time there, I was living the double life, leaving her alone as I traveled back to Idaho for weeks at a time to continue training with Sloan. I took aim at the '99 World Championships but had to pull out after knee surgery. I trained for the 2000 Olympics but ruptured my plantar two weeks before the trials. Shortly thereafter, I had to look in the mirror. There was no official retirement. But I knew I was done.

In 2002 I moved to Arizona full time. I also married Leilani in Hawaii, which will forever be the best decision of my life. But still, I was searching. I had millions of dollars, a beautiful wife, a gold medal and absolutely no idea what to do next. For a period in my life, I woke up every morning knowing exactly

Dan and Leilani O'Brien

what I was trying to do. I had a clear purpose, and now I didn't. People like Milt say a man without purpose is a man without direction, and a man without direction is never far from losing his way. I believe it, because it happened to me once before.

And it was starting to happen again.

I went back to drinking. It started out on the weekends, relaxing by the pool, out at the golf course, but suddenly being at the pool and the golf course was becoming my whole life. It felt like I was on a permanent vacation, which probably sounds great to most people, but to me it was a trap, an open invitation to the re-emergence of my every weakness. Pretty soon I was drinking on the weekdays, and before long I was doing it every day. I let three years go by with absolutely nothing to show for them. My money was evaporating. My marriage was shaky at best.

I say to Brad, "When you're driving home from the casino at four in the morning with one eye open, that's when you've got a problem."

"So what did you do?" he asks.

"I started going to some AA meetings. I had to stand up and admit some things."

"And did it help?"

As I go on to tell Brad, yeah, I think it did help. I started to scale the drinking back. But then, I don't think my drinking has ever actually been the main problem. I think, like I've said a hundred times, my greatest strength is my greatest weakness. When I decide to do something, I'm full throttle. For a long time I channeled this extremism into a good thing, and it took me a long way. Every day I felt inspired by the thrill of the chase, and now, I was desperate for that feeling again. So I began to search for absolutely anything to serve as that carrot to go after. I decided to rent a building and start a gym, thinking that owning a business might do the trick. It didn't. It was a money pit.

"And the worst part is," I tell Brad, "I didn't even really listen to Lei on the idea."

"Did she think it was a bad idea?"

"Absolutely," I say. "But that was the thing: I was always living for me, and she and everyone else in my life sort of rode in the backseat. A driven man is a selfish man, and for a long time I was the height of both. To look back at the stuff I put her through makes me feel awful in a way I can't even describe."

In 2006, with my life spiraling, I finally found my way back to the track, becoming a volunteer assistant coach at ASU, and pretty quickly, as I worked alongside these young athletes and watched them chase their dreams, it started to reinvigorate my passion. I'd jump right in the discus ring and throw with the guys. Shot puts. Pole vaults. It really gave me a high to be working hard again. But is it possible that being back around the track, in a small way, was also serving as a daily reminder of the one thing I could no longer do? The only thing I ever really wanted to do?

I only ask this because for all the inspiration that was suddenly coming back into my life, a part of me was still longing, even aching, for something more. Whether it was my duties at ASU, my television gigs, my business endeavors, I couldn't wholly commit myself to any one thing. "Still," I told Brad, "everything came back to Milt's question. Everything always comes back to that question. What do I want? The day I stopped competing was the day I stopped being able to answer that question, and to this day, I still can't answer it."

Three days after I tell Brad this, he shows up at my house.

"You got a minute?"

"Sure, man. What's up?"

We go into the kitchen. Sit down at the table. Brad's got a proposal.

"So I've been thinking about what you said, about the question that Milt asked you that day. And it's made me realize that I've never fully figured out what I want."

I lean in. This is important stuff.

"I want to be an author," he says. "I want to write books. I want to tell stories that really matter, and I think your story matters. I see the way it affects people at your speeches, and I know the way it's affected me. Have you ever thought about writing a book? I think I could help you do a good job."

Wow. That caught me a little off guard. But to hear the passion in Brad's voice, I feel an immediate twinge of my own inspiration. The truth is, I have thought about writing a book before. In fact, shortly after the Olympics a guy came to Idaho and started following me around, but it never materialized. And to be honest, that was a good thing. I wasn't ready to tell my story yet, at least not with any sort of honesty or perspective. But I do think I'm ready now. I do have some things to say. I do think that taking an honest look back might be a big step in my ongoing mission to move forward. And after reading the article Brad wrote on me, yeah, I absolutely do think he's the right guy to help me. Suddenly it feels like fate, like Brad got assigned that article for a reason, like he and I crossed paths at a time when we were both ready to do something.

"You know what," I say, "let's do it."

"Really?" he says excitedly. "You mean it?"

"Absolutely, man. I'm all in."

And so it begins. A week later Brad comes over with a blank legal pad and a tape recorder, and we go to work. Neither of us have done this before, so in most every way we don't have a clue what we're doing. We don't know how to structure the story. We don't know where to start it. We don't know whether to go first person or third person, past or present tense. But slowly, together, we're starting to figure it out.

It's not easy getting into the details of my life. I have to face up to some things I'm not proud of. The idiot I was in college. The way I pissed on chances people gave me.

I tell Brad how I always felt a little bit alone and in some ways still do. I tell him that my biological parents were never found, that all the letters and database searches came up empty and I'm OK with that. I've always been grateful for the family that I have.

It's not lost on me that when I started out, I had no family at all. I had my first two birthdays in orphanages. And yet I wound up with the biggest family a kid could ever want. Not only that, but I feel like I'm a part of Coach Sloan's family and Coach Keller's family. I have three towns that have taken me in as their own. I am humbled to be a part of the decathlon fraternity. I'll never forget the day Bruce Jenner turned to me and said, "Welcome to the club, kid." And most important of all, I have this little family of mine in Arizona—Leilani and our two dogs, Max and Kina. Telling this story is reminding me of all the wonderful people and things in my life, and that it's coming across so authentically on the page is really exciting. We feel like we have a good thing going here. We find an agent. We land a small publishing deal. We're cruising along with the wind at our backs, 40,000 words scattered about and outlines in place. And then, suddenly, everything hits the skids.

"Dude," Brad says, "I'm moving to Florida."

"You're what?"

"I got that job with CBS Sports. I'm moving to Florida in a month."

I know he's been interviewing, but this still feels out of nowhere. I'm happy for him. It's a good job that he's worked for. But as we're about to find out, this isn't doing the book any favors. We don't live 10 minutes from each other anymore. We can't go to the gym or the golf course and chat for hours.

Meanwhile, my schedule is cramming up like a hoarder's closet, and I don't find that coincidental. In working on this book, in literally closing off my past one chapter at a time, both good and bad, I'm starting to move forward with an excitement I haven't felt in years. I'm pursuing business opportunities that I let slide by in the past. I'm working with Yahoo for the 2012 Olympics. I've signed on with Andre Agassi and Gil Reyes to help endorse the new line of strength equipment they've launched. And I'm involving Lei in every decision. I don't want to live *with* her anymore. I want to live *for* her.

But the book is suffering. There's no time. I'm traveling everywhere, and Brad is suddenly working until two in the morning. We're trying. We don't want the story to fall short of what we hoped it would be. But we're failing. Badly. We miss one deadline. Two deadlines. Three deadlines. Brad's working into the wee hours, running on basically no sleep for months, and the time difference is a nightmare. I'm setting my alarm for 3 a.m. to get up and read drafts and make changes so Brad can have a few hours before work to re-write, but it's wearing us to the bone.

One night Brad calls me, "Dude," he says, "I don't think I'm cut out to write books."

I get pissed. "Don't ever let me hear you say that again. This is your dream. You're doing this."

"But it's so hard, man. I'm completely exhausted."

"I know you are. So am I. But nothing worth doing is easy. This is the grind of it."

Suddenly, every lesson that I've ever learned, every piece of advice that was ever given to me by Sloan or Milt or anyone else, I'm now passing on to Brad. And in that shift, in that role reversal, a transformation that's been slowly happening for the last few years is finally becoming complete. I'm no longer the dreamer anymore. I'm the one who wants to inspire the dreamer. I've become Milt. And it's making me feel happy. Fulfilled.

To work with my athletes at ASU gives me purpose. To train 15-year-old Gregory Anderson, the No. 2-ranked tennis player from his age group in the Southwest, gives me purpose. If Milt were to show up on my doorstep tomorrow and ask me what I want, for the first time in a very, very long time, I could look him right in the eye, with absolutely certainty, and tell him that I want to inspire other people to pursue what they want in life. I've accepted that it's not my turn anymore. It's Gregory's turn. It's Alex Wentz's turn, a decathlete I trained with at ASU, who fulfilled his dream of becoming a marine.

This book is an ending for me but a beginning for Brad. He wants to do this for the rest of his life, and we can't stop now. I tell him to push. I send him texts telling him it's never as bad as it seems. We finish off chapter after chapter. We're getting close. It feels like we're stuck in the longest 1500-meter of my life. We're tired. We're under pressure. We're making it harder than it is. We'd give anything in the world to be doing anything else. But now we're one chapter away, one lap away, and anyone can do anything one more time. We push through the last wall and hit a second wind somewhere in the middle of another 40-hour session that we can hardly remember, and when we cross the final T, when we attach the book in an email and finally send it off to the publisher, we do not feel joy or satisfaction. We feel only relief.

"We did it," I tell Brad from Arizona. "We finished."

He can't even say anything on the other end. For five seconds it's silent.

"Brad? You there?"

"Barely," he says, mustering a tiny laugh. "Barely."

And really, that's all we can say. We're too tired to say anything else. If this book has proved nothing else, if we sell 10 copies to nobody but our families, it has shown that life truly is a decathlon. It's not about winning and losing. It's about proving something to yourself. It's about proving that if you want something badly enough, if you're willing to sacrifice, you can overcome the struggle and the pain and you can get through. And in that quest, in that intimidating task of finding your passion and pursuing it to the very limit and beyond, lies our only true fulfillment.

So in the end, I will continue to go to the track. I will continue to climb stairs and run sprints with the absolute determination and joy of a man whose next event is right around the corner. I will do this not because I don't know how to do anything else, but rather because I don't *want* to do anything else. This is who I am. This is who I'll always be. I will push myself as an athlete so that I can push myself as a man, as a husband, as a son, as a friend. For in the words I once heard from the great Milt Campbell, "Good better best. Never rest. Until the good gets better, and the better gets best."